I0426829

a division of Clark Schpiell Productions
www.randomwerewolf.com

designed by David Nett

WE and GWB

notes from the first four years

david nett • jeanette scherrer
jeremy groce • joseph g. carson
craig bridger • chad schnaible
rick robinson • michelle magoffin
& eli chartkoff

edited by: nikki lee & david nett

For Judy and Grandpa Nett,
who helped to teach us right from wrong.
We hope we learned our lessons well.

Contents

Introduction

On November 2, 2000, I was in rehearsal for the first play produced by what would later become Lucid by Proxy (the theater company run by Shannon [my wife], me, and a handful of my close friends, including Jeanette and Rick, both of whom have contributed to this book). While Shannon and I were driving to Rick's house (where the rehearsal was to take place), Florida was called for Gore. By the time we walked into Rick's living room, it was being called for Bush. Halfway through rehearsal, no one seemed to know who would win Florida's crucial votes, but it appeared to be leaning toward Gore. By the time rehearsal was over, FOX News, and others, had started calling it for Bush again.

That night was the first time I heard someone (my good friend John) say that if Bush were elected, he'd move to Canada. We all laughed, and agreed. But none of us really meant it. The election was disappointing, and none of us understood how this man, who most of us saw as simply an underqualified clown, could have defeated Vice President Gore. We worried about what this might mean for the environment, for the economy (Bush was already talking up his proposed tax cuts), and for abortion and stem cell research. Beyond that, though, we did not conceive of the serious damage this smirking, jovial, again, *clownish* man could do to our country.

The first few essays that appeared in our online magazine, *Clark Schpiell Productions,* about President Bush and politics under his administration were humorous – light political satire aimed at a president who was a poor public speaker and who had a history of deferring to his handlers. We were, after all, primarily an online humor magazine, or at least we were trying to be. Most of our content consisted of satire, scatalogical humor, and the occaisional book or film review.

After September 11, 2001, that began to slowly change. More and more, essays focused on politics. More and more, the handful of writers who contributed to the site started to grasp the seriousness of the damage George

W. Bush could do to America and her ideals and place in the world. More and more, these regular, mostly historically non-political folk began to respond in the best way they knew how – by writing about what, in their minds, was going terribly wrong. *Clark Schpiell Productions*, a tiny online humor magazine, began to transform.

This is the record of that transformation; how a handful of regular folks (most of us, for our day jobs, are cubicle jockeys) began to understand the impact of the first George W. Bush administration on the future of America, and how we tried, in our small way, to change things.

David Nett
Editor, Contributor & Webmaster
Clark Schpiell Productions
December 17, 2004

Kansas Curriculum Gems

David Nett   February 21, 2001

L ast week the Kansas State School Board reluctantly made the
monumental decision to allow Darwin's widely accepted (for the last
75 years or so) Theory of Evolution back into its schools' core science
curriculum. A couple of the Board's members steadfastly objected to the
decision, declaring evolution merely one of many theories available to
modern biologists, and that the theory is not so widely accepted as many
would believe, especially among the bush-people of the Serengeti and creepy
banjo-playing kids in the Appalachian mountains.

While the whole evolution thing got a lot of press, many other minor
changes were also made to the curriculum, at the behest of reported "hippies
and science-lovers:"

Physical Science Core, part 5.3

While the well-respected Kansas State School Board does still contend
that, in having one's picture taken, the camera does, in fact, steal one's soul,
the School Board can no longer condone restoring the soul by burning the
film and/or polaroid picture in a fire of fragrant sandalwood and breathing
deeply of the smoke. Please note that this does not constitute a full reversal
in policy, it is merely a change to placate the so called "State Fire Marshall"
in his insistence that fires be prohibited on school grounds. The non-fire
related destruction of Digital Cameras, which can steal the soul as well
and, since no physical image exists, cause the soul to be irretrievably lost, is
still advisable and encouraged, however, along with all computers within
"transmission range."

Biology Core, Part 17.0

When someone sneezes, his or her soul vacates the body for a few
seconds – no one can reasonably dispute this fact. However, because of
the separation of church and state (which the KSSB reluctantly defends),
students should not say "God Bless You" to protect the exposed soul.

Rather, students should encircle the congested student in a ring of purifying fire which may protect against the horned one. (Since fires are officially discouraged on school grounds, please limit sneezing to non-school areas for maximum soul-protection.)

American History Core, Part 79.33

Former President Bill Clinton most likely is not, as suggested in previous curriculum, Lucifer, Lord of Hell, in disguise. Lucifer would surely have been able to place his successor in the seat of the presidency, especially when running against such a pudding-head. It is more probable he is simply a minor demon, sent to wreak havoc on the morals of America.

Geology Core, Part 7.6.6

"Deep within these caves at the center of the Earth live the Morlocks and the Nevebezzers, two nefarious warring species of highly-intelligent humanoids whose constant feuding will surely eventually burst forth onto the surface and spell mankind's doom." [*note: Previously, "Nevebezzers" had been misspelled.*]

Our first attempt at a participatory political message on Clark Schpiell Productions met with a resounding silence, save for one response from my friend Bob Brewer, to whom I don't even remember talking about the site. In retrospect, it was perhaps an overly optimistic attempt at engaging our readers, considering we were, at that time, receiving maybe 300 visits per week, if we were lucky. The fact that even one of those responded, friend or no, was a minor miracle.

Ashamed of the small response, I never published the promised follow-up. Sorry, Bob.

I'm Sorry, So Sorry

David Nett   April 8, 2001

We all know the story. Our spy plane buzzes around international airspace that China claims as theirs. China sends up a coupla fighter planes to buzz our plane. Our plane and one of theirs collide. The fighter dumps in the ocean, and our plane lands on Chinese soil. And now China has had our 24 servicemen in its custody for a week and one day.

I'm not gonna argue about who was right, or about who caused the crash or for what reasons. But I am gonna point out that all China wants from us, in exchange for our servicemen, is an apology. And, while our government has to worry about such things as "National Honor" and saving face in front of the rest of the nations of the world, allies and enemies alike, we have no such constraints. In fact, just the opposite – we all know that we routinely make asses of ourselves, in front of friends, enemies, and the entire customer base of the Whittier TGIFriday's last Wednesday around 10:15PM.

So, while our leaders' hands are tied, ours (unless you count that 45 minutes a few weeks ago in the privacy of our own homes where we can do whatever we damn well please) are not. *Clark Schpiell Productions* is proud to offer the citizens of this country a chance to step up and do what our leaders cannot: apologize to China.

Just fill in the form below and apologize for whatever you feel is necessary. You don't have to mean it – China will never know. In a week or two, we'll post the best of the apologies on our website, which is regularly visited by Chinese President Jiang Zemin (as well as many other foreign heads of state and various dignitaries).

C'mon, step up. To quote Peter Frechette as Louis DiMucci from the critically acclaimed 80's film, *Grease2*, "Let's do it for our country!"

Die, McVeigh, Die

David Nett   June 11, 2001

Timothy McVeigh was put to death at 7:15 this morning, Central Daylight Time, by the federal government of the United States of America. He was convicted of crimes related to the terrorist bombing of the Oklahoma City Federal Building, and the of killing 168 people (169, if you believe *Salon.com*'s assertion that there was an extra leg in the rubble that didn't belong to anyone). And if you don't know any of this, you've been living in a hole since before April, 1995.

I'm not going to sway anyone on the merits of the death penalty here. Those who are for the death penalty are generally strongly for it, those opposed are passionately opposed – no minds would be changed by a short *CSP* article. And, while I personally oppose the death penalty, even I find it hard to object to the humane and relatively painless execution of a man who admits to having killed 168 people. What I do object to, what does make me most sad, is the rabidity with which we as a people killed this man. From the "Buh-bye Tim" signs on peoples' lawns, to the cheering and hollering on various radio morning shows, it is evident we took great pleasure in this very public execution.

While the 1967 film *Hang'em High* isn't among Clint Eastwood's best, the last half hour of it has stuck with me since the first time I saw it, in maybe 4th or 5th grade. After Marshall Jeddediah Cooper rounds up a band of cattle rustlers and helps (against his will) to get them convicted and sentenced to hanging, the town and the surrounding countryside go into a kind of frenzy. People travel from miles in every direction to see the hanging of 6 men at once – among them, two teenaged boys. The town's inns fill to overflowing, people are camped in wagons and makeshift tents all around the outskirts, and the saloons are packed with drunken revelers. When the day of the hanging comes, the town square is packed shoulder to shoulder with screaming people – men, women and children. Beverage and food vendors hawk their wares to the rabid crowd, and even the whorehouse closes as the prostitutes join the crowd of spectators. The scene is ugly and dirty, and it is supposed to be. The plot calls for it – Clint's character has been unfairly lynched in his past, and he is remorseful. And the movie audience needs it to be ugly – we need to see a definite difference between that crowd and us. We need to be shown that the idea that people would cheerfully gather to watch other men die is primitive and repugnant, that it could never happen in modern times, that our evolved American society is beyond such base expressions of delight in another man's death.

The truth is, given the right cause, we are still that same mob. Given a man who is clearly guilty, who has attacked the country as a whole, who has killed not only adults, but children, too, and admitted to it, we are that mob. We collectively booed when McVeigh's execution was delayed so that time could be taken to weigh the recently uncovered FBI evidence. We celebrated when a federal judge declared that the evidence would not have changed the outcome of the trial, and that the execution could be carried out as planned. We did our best to try to get the execution broadcast via network television, cable television, pay-per-view television, the internet. Barring that, we tried to videotape the damn thing so we could see it later, under whatever context a judge might let the viewing happen. And, this morning we hooted and hollered and sent each other emails with a picture of a blackened piece of toast in the shape of a man attached and played exaggerated frying sounds over the radio (even though McVeigh died by lethal injection, not by electrocution).

This morning, President Bush said, "Today every living person who was hurt by the evil done in Oklahoma City can rest in the knowledge that there has been a reckoning." He also said that "good overcomes evil." I hope he's right. But, again, looking at us, at the way many of us have acted in recent weeks and months – the drunk frat boys howling at *Faces of Death IV*, the farmers and ranchers crowded around to watch the hanging – I just don't know what to make of all this. Antonio Maria Pereira, a Portuguese civil rights activist, said "The death penalty is a barbarism inappropriate to our times." Like I said earlier, I'm not going to argue the merits of capital punishment itself. But the way many have acted towards the execution can only be called barbaric.

I don't want to seem like I'm condemning the American people as a whole. Not all of us celebrated, of course, at least not this outwardly. In fact, I'm certain most Americans probably felt a little uncomfortable at the celebration of the rest, and looked away. But it still makes me cold inside, and sad. A few of us had courage enough to protest this seemingly unprotest-able event, but they protested against the death penalty, not against the seeming joy with which proponents of the execution carried it out. I think that, even for proponents of the death penalty, each execution should be a somber, sobering event. When a life is taken, no matter how repugnant we might view that life, we should not celebrate.

A group of people standing outside the prison in Indiana this morning chanted "die, McVeigh, die," and "this is for Oklahoma City." But, I don't think all of this was *for* anything. Mostly, I think, it was *against* us.

On the morning of September 11, 2001, Shannon's dad called us and told us to turn on the television. We, like so many thousands of Americans, were watching live when the second plane hit the towers. Even though we were in Los Angeles, it all seemed very, scarily close.

I didn't lose anyone close to me in that attack, which is pointed out to me whenever I argue against the myriad ways that event has been exploited for political gain in the past few years. I was particularly upset by the "not in our back yard" posters which immediately popped up all over, including in my place of work. The implication that terrorism against other people is fine, but when you fuck with Americans, boy-howdy, that's a different story, is disgusting. Terrorism existed before 9/11. We just weren't paying attention. I'm a proud American, but American lives are not more important than any other lives.

My heart goes out to everyone who did experience first-hand that terrible loss, to the American soldiers who lost their lives defending their country and executing their sworn duties, and to the countless innocents who have since faced the business-end of our retaliation.

Unsurprisingly, most of our political discussion over the next several months focused on 9/11 and its immediate consequences.

Nostradamus Nonsense

David Nett   September 14, 2001

O kay, I'm sick of getting frigging email about how Nostradamus
predicted last week's tragic events. About eight different people
have sent it to me – you've probably gotten it, too. If you haven't, I suspect
sometime soon you'll see an email in your inbox that describes how
Nostradamus predicted the terrorist attacks on the U.S., supposedly proven
by this quote:

> "In the City of God there will be a great thunder, two brothers torn
> apart by chaos, while the fortress endures, the great leader will
> succumb."

> "The third big war will begin when the big city is burning."

> "On the 11th day of the 9th month that...two metal birds would crash
> into two tall statues...in the new city...and the world will end soon
> after"

> Nostradamus – 1654

Sick of receiving this crap every time anything bad happens (and,
specifically, sick of this particular email), I immediately set out to debunk it,
in vain hope that I could break the chain (from the seven further versions
I received, it is clear I was not successful). I spent a few hours and found a
good, thorough (English – unfortunately I don't read French) electronic text
version of all 10 centuries of Nostradamus predictions (all in four-line verses
called "quatrains"). I then did a thorough (computerized – I didn't read them
all) search of all of the quatrains.

First off, Nostradamus' predictions were, as stated above, in the form
of quatrains. These quatrains are arranged into groups of 100 for each of
10 centuries (except for, I think, century XIII, which has only 43 quatrains).
Each quatrain is a separate entity – a separate prediction – which relates to
that specific century. Taking chunks from several quatrains, possibly across
several centuries, as has been done in this "quote," makes no sense at all. Nor

does replacing words with ellipses (...), as each word has meaning. Replacing or removing words only further indicates that someone is attempting to bend a quote to another meaning. Because of this manipulation alone, the quote is extremely suspect.

Delving in further, while I can find 5 references to the "New City," none of them involve metal birds or two tall statues. All quotes I can find that refer to the 11th day of the "sept" month (probably, according to most analysis, the Julian Calendar seventh month, which would be our Gregorian Calendar's August or September) refer to the "99th year," commonly thought to be 1999. Our current year, 2001, is not mentioned along with that "sept 11."

In addition, I find no references at all to "metal birds" or "two tall statues." Translations from the old French are often inaccurate, but it seems unlikely that I would find none of these many things purely by mistake of translation. It is more likely that the quote here comes from a very broad interpretation of a quatrain, a mistaken translation, or is simply entirely made-up.

Based on all of this, I'm certain this email is sensationalist bunk. Even if you do believe in Nostradamus' predictive abilities, it appears that this "quote" is mis-represented, and may not even actually be taken from parts of Nostradamus' already nebulous predictions. Why anyone would make this stuff up, I'm not certain. It doesn't help anyone deal with this tragedy, and I can't find any self-promotional angle. Maybe it comes from someone who just gets off on having his/her email flood everyone's inbox.

A Measured Response

David Nett   September 17, 2001

I spent a lot of time this weekend outside of my home. My wife and I attended funeral services for a dear friend on Saturday (her death, though tragic, was not connected with last week's terrorist attacks). We also went to the L.A. County Fair this weekend, in an attempt to get our minds off of our national and personal tragedies, and ran numerous errands at various stores around the city, trying as much as possible to return to normalcy.

As we walked through crowds of people all weekend, I cannot begin to count the number of times I heard people declaring, at the top of their lungs, that we should bomb the bejeezus out of Afghanistan and other Arabic countries. "Nuke 'em," "turn it into a sea of glass," "bomb them back to the stone age." some of these comments came from friends, and once even from a dear friend – a playwright whom I admire and look to as a mentor. I'd been hearing these same comments from my co-workers all week and, as the weekend wore on, I began to feel sick. Where did this bloodthirstiness come from? How did the people around me, people I love and respect, become so full of hate?

Make no mistake, I am stunned, saddened and furious over the attacks of last Tuesday. I am lucky in that none of my friends or relatives were killed in the four crashes. But I am outraged at the attack against my country, and, even more, at the attack against the human race. These attacks were more than a declaration of war against the US, they were a boldfaced rejection of the idea that human life is important, that each person has a purpose and the right to do his or her work on this earth. I find it inconceivable that anyone should undertake such a slaughter in the name of God (I'm certain many will write about that – I'll leave it alone), and even more inconceivable that any man or woman could look at the faces around him, could picture the faces of teeming thousands simply going about their work, and choose to kill them all. I think that most all of my friends, co-workers and, indeed, the people in those throngs that I walked through this weekend, would feel the same way, which is why I am baffled by those comments.

As the smell of death blows through New York City and Washington D.C., as men and dogs risk their lives to pull bodies and body parts from the smoldering wreckage of some of our greatest engineering marvels, I am at a loss to understand how anyone could call for more violence. Looking at the devastation caused by this attack on us, really looking at it as we have for the past week, can anyone say they honestly would like to see more of it? Do we want to see more cities devastated, more countries brought to their knees, more pieces of human bodies blown through busy streets, more rescue workers crushed by falling buildings while trying to do nothing more than save the fallen? Even if all this happens in some other country, in someone else's "back yard?"

If we want to show the world that we intend to right the wrongs of the past week, that we intend to protect and preserve the freedoms and rights that we see as being part of the American way of life, we must do so with deliberation, awareness, and restraint. If indeed Osama Bin Laden is the orchestrator of this attack, he should be tried and brought to justice in just the same way as other war criminals and creators of such atrocities are brought to justice. If we want to truly protect the things that America stands for – human rights and due process among them – we need to extend the initiators of these attacks those same rights and courtesies. If we retaliate with missiles, bombs, tanks and planes; if we kill tens or hundreds or thousands of innocents in our quest for vengeance, then our attackers will have won their war. Our attackers will have destroyed our sense of who we are and what we stand for, and will have reduced us to their level, which is exactly what they want. If we want to set an example for the world, we will defend ourselves with reason and righteous indignation. Certainly, in all of this, there are those who deserve death, and worse, for what has been done. But if we can rise above the simple, primitive joy of killing our enemies, we will be all the more the victors in this war.

The slaughter of countless thousands more innocents will accomplish nothing, or next to it, especially considering the loose organization of our new enemies. Only by rising above their apparent disdain for human life, by executing justice, with support of our allies, in a reasoned manner and only against those who are clearly guilty, as is the American way, can we hope to preserve the rights and ideals that Americans and nearly all the western world hold dear.

I think that should be our goal. Let us not turn Afghanistan into a "sea of glass." Let us instead show those who attacked us, and other would-be terrorists, that the American spirit is grand and righteous, and that we love human life as much as we despise our enemies. Let us take our example from Gandhi and Martin Luther King, Jr., not from the Crusades or our military textbooks. Our losses were horrible, and our hearts must go out to everyone who lost a loved one, and we must do what we can to help them. Last week's battle, humanity clearly lost. But, if we are careful, certainly humanity can win the war.

Red Robot is a character created by Sam Brown of the amazing "Exploding Dog" (www.explodingdog.com).

He also appears frequently in Richard Stevens' fantastic webcomic "Diesel Sweeties" (www.dieselsweeties.com), and throughout the Dumbrella web network (www.dumbrella.com).

President Bush Ups the Ante

David Nett   September 30, 2001

In a surprising move yesterday afternoon, U.S. President George W. Bush took another step in the escalation of his war on terrorism. On top of calling up thousands of reservists, sending troops and military machines into the Middle East, freezing the assets of suspected terrorists and renaming his war project "Enduring Freedom," Bush dramatically upped the serious-o-meter of his activities by calling on the patriotism of Red Robot.

"All Americans must do their part," declared the President. "I think Red Robot is an American. He's red. That's one of our three American colors. And he's got blinking blue and white diodes inside his metal belly. Or so I've imagined. How much more American can you get?"

Bush went on to sketch out the role he imagined Red Robot playing in America's near future. "He'll use his rocket pack to fly over the Hindu Kush mountains, thereby circumventing the dangerously unpredictable weather and multiple ambush opportunities of the Khyber Pass, while avoiding radar, since his physical profile is much smaller than that of conventional aircraft," Bush stated, while illustrating with a sweeping gesture the plan he'd drawn in green crayon on the Oval Office wall. "He'll then touch down at the nearest of Bin Laden's terrorist training camps and wreak his terrible metal havoc!"

"Afterward," he said, "he'll wave his arms frantically and say 'Danger, Bin Laden-son, Danger!'"

Secretary of Defense Donald Rumsfeld wept softly throughout the presentation.

When pressed for further details and long term plans for Red Robot, and how the Administration felt about utilizing the skills of an entity often accused of crushing people without cause, and who has often attempted World Domination himself, Bush ran into the Oval Office bathroom and locked the door.

Red Robot was reached for comment on the steps of the Marin County Courthouse, where he'd just been found "not guilty" of the crushing of seven people by reason of gross mechanical failure.

"I do not know this hu-man, George Bush," said Red Robot. "But I cannot be ruled by any meat-creatures. I crush all hu-mans indiscriminately. I do not single out any one hu-man or group of hu-mans for crushing. Except perhaps for Pat Robertson and Jerry Falwell – them I single out. Laying the blame for the terrorist attacks on homosexuals and pro-choice groups raises my fearsome digital ire."

Pat Robertson and Jerry Falwell could not be reached for comment.

Modern Warfare
or, Responsibility and the War on Terrorism

Jeremy Groce   September 30, 2001

September 11th was a day that put most of the country into a state of profound shock, a sensation that isn't felt too often in a nation with 24/7 news coverage that ignores most of the world. But because this horrific event happened here at home, we were stunned, saddened, and angered to a degree rarely experienced in the United States in the past 100 years.

I'm not that interested in talking about the tragedy itself. Reflections on the dead and the presumed dead are best left to poets and pastors. I also don't want to talk about "how this could have happened," the apparent lapses in safety and security at our nation's largest airports, or the "failure in intelligence" that politicians will debate.

What I want to discuss is how we should proceed: what should we do next? Polls taken in the days since the terrorist attacks have shown overwhelming support for a strong military retaliation. That's understandable. I imagine no shortage of volunteers would be willing to track down those responsible for the planning (if not direct execution) of these attacks and personally strangle them dead. But a purely violent response on our part could escalate tensions between the West (particularly the United States) and even friendly (or at least not unfriendly) Arab and Islamic states. In the end, we can all agree that above all else we want to end terrorism. And to do that, the causes of terrorism must be understood and addressed.

The goal of "ending terrorism" is ostensibly the overarching objective of the "new war" that President Bush and, it seems, the entire Washington D.C. administration, intends to pursue. Ending terrorism is a lofty objective, but how realistic a goal is it? To answer this question, let's talk about some other "wars" that we're involved in at the moment.

Since crack became a common narcotic in this country, the government has waged a War on Drugs. Our government spends billions every year in the effort to halt the creation and distribution of illegal substances. The problem is that drugs themselves aren't really the issue. Drugs don't attack. Drugs don't sneak into the country. Drugs don't manufacture themselves. People are responsible for the creation, distribution, and consumption of drugs. And as long as there are consumers, there will be manufacturers. To attempt to stop one without the other is folly. In a real war, a victor is declared when their opposition surrenders or dies. How will we know the war on drugs is over? When all people in the drug trade – users and manufacturers – are dead? When every last dealer turns themselves in to the police?

The United States has also, at times in our recent history, fought wars on crime. But crime has never and will never go away. Poverty, misery, even psychosis will always drive some people to commit crimes. How can crime be eliminated if its causes cannot be?

A war on terrorism could be as pointless and impossible to win as the wars on drugs and crime. Terrorists may not be as intangible as drugs, nor as common as criminals, but they are not a single political or geopolitical entity with an easily identifiable leadership that can be destroyed and eliminated. We may be able to capture, even kill, Osama bin Laden, but he is not the only radical Islamic fundamentalist obsessed with the destruction of the United States.

It's also important to consider that the men who committed the September 11th attacks weren't just terrorists. They were suicide terrorists. These men were not only willing, but eager, to die for their cause. What deterrence can we have to this kind of zealot? What makes someone willing to kill himself for a cause? The primary reason is a religious one. Someone is convincingly telling these young men that their sacrifices will take them directly to heaven.

Why would someone be so anxious to end life on this world and go to the next one? The answer lies in the day-to-day living conditions of the typical terrorist recruit. Thousands of Palestinians in the Middle East, in particular, live in refugee camps in the West Bank and Gaza Strip. The camps are filthy, disease-ridden, and crowded. Job and educational opportunities are extremely limited – virtually non-existent. They see Israel and Israelis as the obstacles to any improvement of their lives. If a young man growing up in a Palestinian refugee camp, or in Lebanon or Afghanistan, can be convinced that blowing himself up in a crowded restaurant or slamming himself and his vehicle into a structure full of Americans will not only take him to heaven, it will give his family and friends a better chance of escaping the misery and suffering of their daily lives, then what can really be done to stop him?

To end terrorism, we need to acknowledge this reality. While nothing justifies or excuses the terrorists' attacks, we still have a responsibility to do our part to actively create a true, just peace in the Middle East. Many terrorists believe Israel couldn't exist without the U.S.'s support. If we openly favor Israel, as our government tends to do, the Arab world will not trust us to be involved in enforcing any peace. Palestinians, Lebanese, and Afghans must see an improvement in their lives so that desperate acts of terrorism aren't viewed as promising releases from pain. At the same time, the Arab world must be willing to compromise and accept on some level the right for Israel to exist. Israel must acknowledge that their nation was created out of land that didn't belong to them and modify their society accordingly.

We must rethink our role in the world and act less unilaterally. We should act only when invited or when our direct national security is threatened, or when there exists a true international consensus that action must be taken.

We must also realize that as the wealthiest, most powerful nation on Earth, there will always be people and groups who hate us and would like to see us destroyed. And for this reason we must defend ourselves. Defense, in fact, is the most important response at the moment. Just as you lock your doors to defend yourself from crime and you educate your children as a defense against drug abuse, we must take measures to defend ourselves from terrorism. The trick will be doing this without stripping ourselves of our civil liberties.

Of course, the suggestions I've outlined here will require a great deal of work and a great deal of cooperation and compromise among many disparate groups. They may seem impossible to realize. Surely they are no more impossible than a victory in a war "to rid the world of evil." If creating a world without terror is truly our intent, let our actions achieve justice and not more pain and suffering.

What Hasn't Changed in America

Joseph G. Carson   October 15, 2001

A bout forty-eight seconds after the initial attack on September 11th, the news media leapt into a breach of intellectual discourse in which they love to engage: instantly casting forward into the future and talking about the import of the events currently unfolding, or, as I like to call it, "pre-historicization." The bit they most harped on was that everything had changed. Every last damn thing about America was now completely different. Frogs had become birds; men had become women; there would never be another violent movie again; people would appreciate the little things in life like they had never done in the history of mankind.

This seemed a bit extreme for my tastes, and I admit to disliking change, especially when it involves biological warfare, religion, and damn well everything! So, to calm myself, in the past month I've set out to find ways in which life is still exactly the same, and I was surprised and, yay, comforted by the fact that some routines and modes of life in this country seem inviolable. I offer up the following list for your spiritual and emotional sustenance.

- My cat still persists in yowling like an abused infant whenever I wake up and hence become available to give her the food she has been wickedly denied by my slumber. I have tried to explain to her that in light of September 11, her continual howling when she is, in fact, rather plump, could strike many as insensitive to the newfound understanding and somber profundity we are now in. This lecture, I might add, does absolutely nothing to appease her.

- Americans are still, by and large, despite being the nation with the most automobiles in the history of mankind, still unable to operate certain fundamental pieces of said machinery, the turn signal being a prominent example.

- Irony, despite what one is reading in the pop sociology rags, seems to be persisting, though I believe it should perish and recently admonished a fellow employee, who had made an ironic comment about the ability or lack thereof of another employee whom we both enjoy despising. I immediately got in his face. "How can you say something like that? Irony is dead, my friend. It died on a single day, September 11th, and never shall it return." He laughed, but I would have none of it. "I'm not kidding." "You're not being sarcastic?" "An even cheaper form of irony!" I huffed. "Not a chance!" He was uneasy then. He retracted his statement and we kept on playing our pinball game. "You're sure you're not kidding?" But I fixed him with such a hot glare that he completely missed his multiball.

- James Joyce's *Ulysses* is still an awfully thick book that would be great to have read, but seems like a lot of work to actually read.

- Americans everywhere are still enjoying the wholesome taste of cheese.

- Michael Jordan is returning to basketball. Have we mentioned that Michael Jordan is the greatest basketball player *in the history of mankind*?

- Once again this year, no one will watch, or care about, the Emmys.

- Americans across this nation still display a determined ignorance of American foreign policy, world history, and non-western cultures and religions.

- On college campuses across this country, countless young men still persist in believing that baseball caps, worn both traditionally and backwards, bespeak suave sophistication and worldliness, and will garner them the finest of honeys.

- Despite airing both before and after September 11th, Americans everywhere continue to find the Carrot Top CALL-ATT commercials profoundly unfunny.

Welcome to the World

Jeremy Groce   October 22, 2001

I've got a little ranting to do about the media and current events. First of all, they're hyping this anthrax in the mail thing like it's the most frightening health and security crisis since the outbreak of HIV/AIDS. Maria Shriver has been filling in for Katie Couric on the *Today Show* this week, and on the morning of October 10th she was the quintessential nasty bitch reporter. She had the postmaster general on that morning, and she demanded of him, "But what are you telling the American people, who are terrified of opening their mail? The letter to Tom Brokaw had no return address; the letter to Tom Daschle had a return address. Should people open mail with no return address or not? Are you just making up guidelines as you go along?" If I were that guy, I'd have given her the finger and walked off the set. But that's me.

Instead, he calmly reviewed the facts. There have been four incidents of anthrax in the mail, out of 20 billion pieces of mail handled by the USPS in the last month. The victims have been very high profile individuals or workers at a controversial media outlet (I'm referring to the tabloid company, though some might include NBC as well). For these reasons, I might have forgiven Maria Shriver if she had admitted that she was terrified of opening her mail, but I've got to tell you: I'm not.

Second, last week I heard a call-in show about "sacrifices during wartime." The point of the program was to debate the kinds of sacrifices Americans should be willing to make during this crisis in our nation. I was interested at first because I thought a discussion of civil liberties might ensue. After all, I think the only reason most people aren't totally freaked out about a lot of the anti-terror measures enacted recently is that (for the most part) we trust our government. We'll see how long the trust lasts if/when any abuses are uncovered.

As it turned out, the program was a forum for people with political bones to pick with the Bush administration. The main guest was calling for a repeal of all tax cuts, increases in other taxes, and he kept quoting FDR! The program even aired a segment of a nationwide broadcast FDR made the night before the D-Day invasion. Let's not compare apples and oranges, all right?

By the time the Japanese surrendered to the Allies in August of 1945, there were some 14 million men and women in the US Armed Services. For nearly four years our troops had fought major foes on two fronts. Major material sacrifices were demanded of our civilian population because our soldiers needed to be clothed, fed, and well supplied.

What comparison can be made with our current "war on terrorism?" Militarily, I doubt we'll ever have more than a few thousand troops in Afghanistan (or elsewhere) at any one time. The terrorists are not the Germans or the Japanese, either, meaning they won't be very capable of mounting major offensives, cutting off supply lines, or disrupting production. So why do I feel like some people think I should start buying "Liberty Bonds" and only eat meat once a week and collect old pots and pans for salvage?

In fact, this is the best time to trim government waste and reduce taxes. Free up as much of the taxpayers' money as possible so we can invest, save, and consume. Instead, Congress and even the Republican president have started spending our tax money like crazy and justifying it all in the name of "homeland defense." Just one of the more egregious examples is the $15 billion dollar handout to the nation's airlines, $5 billion of which is cash. The ridiculous thing is that the airlines say they lost only $1.36 billion in revenues during the federally-mandated shutdown. The rest of the money is just gravy. Now, I agree that it's reasonable for the government to pay the airlines for revenues lost during the FAA-mandated shutdown, but even if I thought it was okay to offset the loss of revenue caused by decreased air travel since September 11th and the subsequent shutdown (and I don't), then I would demand that they maintain their service at pre-September 11th levels. That's not happening, though. Instead, the airlines are cancelling hundreds of flights and laying off thousands of workers – all in order to save even more money.

Airlines ought to be doing what the nation's automakers are doing – offering incentives (read: slashed fares) to travelers to entice them to fly. After all, this country is full of businesses that have been detrimentally affected by the terrorist attacks and the resulting economic anxiety and malaise. Where are their billions from the government?

Clearly there will be a monetary cost to measures that strengthen security – not only in airports, but in many areas and sectors of our society – but most of the costs that we will have to pay will be less tangible ones like time, convenience, and individual liberty.

Third, I heard a sportswriter on the radio this week say that "many people feel [that the US] shouldn't be playing games" in a time like this, meaning that sporting events should be indefinitely postponed. I personally haven't met anyone who has voiced such opinions, but assuming these people are out there, I must ask why.

Security concerns are one thing, but if someone is offended that Americans continue to seek out entertainment in the wake of the September 11th tragedies, then he or she needs to try to put this in some historical perspective.

It's precisely in times like this that entertainment is most needed. People need to have escape from their fears and anxieties. The Great Depression and WWII were boom times for musicians, Vaudeville players and Hollywood moviemakers. In an effort to appear more-somber-than-thou, some Americans and members of the press are giving the terrorists exactly what they want (and this is turning into a cliché, as well).

Let's not forget that 45,000 Americans die every year in automobile accidents, 20,000 or more Americans die every year from the flu, and as many as 400,000 Americans die from smoking-related illnesses every year. If we can just take a deep breath and reflect honestly on our present circumstances, we'll realize that the chances of being blown up by a terrorist or receiving a horrible disease in the mail are incredibly small.

If you have ever traveled to other places in the world, even Europe, you already know that the US is not entering into some brave new world. We are not the first, nor will we be the last, nation to face extremists hell-bent on our destruction. When I lived in Guinea-Bissau in West Africa, police and soldiers had checkpoints all over and stopped cars at random. If you didn't have ID and sometimes a little cash, there was hell to pay. When I lived in Taiwan, occasionally I saw squads of armed soldiers marching through the streets. Policemen carried M-16s. When I was in China, I actually never saw any armed guards, but I'm sure there were plenty of secret police around when I was in Tiananmen Square in Beijing.

The problem is that we deluded ourselves into a false sense of security – hell, false sense of invulnerability – and now we have to face facts. This feeling of vulnerability is unfamiliar, but it should not be paralyzing. It's simply a taste of the reality that most peoples of our world live with. Many peoples' realities are much, much harsher. Let's face this situation like the nation we keep claiming to be – the greatest, strongest on earth – and be mindful of our civil liberties. With luck and perseverance, we'll emerge from this crisis even stronger.

Mostly, as the editor of CSP, I just sit back and await submissions from the other writers (and write essays myself, of course), edit them (very lightly, if at all) and publish them. On very rare occasions I suggest ideas for essays I'd like to see. This is the first political essay I "assigned" to my CSP fellows. I got more than I bargained for (in quality and quantity, especially from Jeremy and Joe).

I published the original in three parts. The first essay contained thoughts from Chad and me, as well as excerpts from Jeremy and Joe's essays, which were published afterward as standalone pieces (parts two & three). Here, part one contains just the content written by Chad and me, with those excerpts removed, since parts two and three follow, and goodness knows you don't wanna read stuff twice — that's just silly.

Biometric Scanning & Civil Rights, Part I

David Nett &
Chad Schnaible

December 3, 2001

Los Angeles is barely a handshake away from installing biometric facial scanners, similar to those used at last year's Super Bowl, in the Los Angeles airport. Other cities are taking the same steps. This is causing some discussion across the country, though (in my humble opinion) not as much as it should. A few of us *CSP*ers weigh in with our thoughts:

David:

It's goofy, I know, and hardly to the point, but the first thing I think when I hear that LAX is a whisper away from installing biometric facial scanners at airport checkpoints is "that's damn cool." And, it is. I mean, we are talking here about machines that can look at your face, scan it, and check that scan against a huge database of facial scans, all in a matter of moments. Just a few years ago, this would have been the stuff of James Bond movies – now it'll be as common and innocuous as airport baggage scanners. So, my geek side takes over, and again I think, "that's damn cool." And, I would be right, if I felt we could trust the scanners to be used in a purely responsible manner. If placed properly, and used by experienced, well-trained individuals without any agenda but the protection of the public, the inconvenience to us would be minimal, and the benefits large. The idea of facial scanning does not make me concerned for myself – I've done nothing wrong, and so most likely have nothing to fear.

But I do worry about how it will affect others, and how the government will leverage the data it gathers on us against our civil liberties. Unfortunately, with the government's recent attempts at the suppression of civil liberties (insistence upon military tribunals, even for citizens, eavesdropping on attorney/client conversations, etc.), I am more worried about the implications of such scanning than I might have been previously. Is data being collected? How long will that data be stored? Who will have access to it? What will be done with it? I tend to be largely trusting of our government (some would say, "naive"), but, after hearing Bush and Ashcroft over the last few weeks, even I am worried. It is hard to stand opposed to any new security measures right now, but we must keep an extremely critical eye toward our leadership, especially in times like these. Facial scanners are just tools, and they are no more insidious than the agendas of the people operating them. It is those agendas against which we should be on our guard.

Chad:

Anytime I hear a phrase such as "biometric facial recognizers," I can't help but think of some stark futuristic world, something akin to *GATTICA*, *Harrison Bergeron*, or *1984*. But, then again, a social security number isn't much more than a human barcode. We are apt to grow accustomed to these things, if implemented in small enough measures. I'm just afraid of what it could develop into. A wall is built brick by brick.

Granted, if the recognizers had been implemented in New York before September 11th, the tragedy may not have taken place. But could you have even imagined such a thing before that date?

In order to allow certain comforts, we must infringe on certain liberties. People kid themselves by thinking we live in a free democracy, but that notion is ludicrous. You can never have a truly free democracy. Our government is as close as it can get, but sheer size alone prevents it from ever being anything more than a restrictive republic. We don't even have much say in what it decides. We, individually, only have a small say in electing the officials that do, and as we found in the last presidential election, even that process can be called into question. If the government doesn't do anything, people claim stoicism and ineffectiveness. If it exercises too much control in order to stop the bleeding, people claim socialism or fascism.

The need for national security is now at heights last seen during the Cold War. The CIA is back in full force and up to its old tricks. Personally, I don't like the idea of full-blown espionage, because that inherently implies spying on your own, but I do like the idea of boarding a plane again without the feeling that it may fly into the White House.

Biometric Scanning & Civil Rights, Part II

Jeremy Groce   October 22, 2001

When it comes to technology and security concerns, I'm of two minds: 1) I feel that any tool which can protect the public-at-large from crime and terrorism is good; 2) I feel that I may live to see the movie *Terminator* become a reality. My challenge, as you can see, is to reconcile the two.

Computers and machines can help police and security forces do things that humans alone cannot do. This is why we devise and employ computers and machines. Let's say we have 250 would-be passengers wanting to board a cross-country flight. Airline and security personnel have (generally) less than 2 hours to search the passengers and all their baggage for potentially dangerous items (which, by the way, now include nail files, plastic forks, rubber mallets, sewing needles, Jackie Chan, and any other object or device which could potentially be used to harm another human being). This is a daunting task and it would be impossible without technology.

On the other hand, I don't think I'm exaggerating to say that within the next few decades we'll have machines that will x-ray, sniff, poke, prod, analyze, inspect, and interrogate you and your bags. These machines will appear first at airports, but could later be placed in shopping malls, sports arenas, restaurants, just about any public place. My wife would probably want to install one at the bedroom door (to be sure I'm not smuggling any latex "weapons" into bed).

Apart from the fact that these machines would probably force us to arrive at any public event hours in advance and open us up to potential embarrassment in front of strangers ("Sir, FBI profiles indicate that only terrorists and criminals have penises *that* small. Would you please step into the back room with Officer Bonglongey?"), there probably isn't anything more to be feared from them than the machines that already exist. After all, your friends probably have a small hidden camera in their bathroom, which means they know you go through their medicine chest and masturbate into their sink. Your local government has probably already installed a camera in the alley behind your favorite restaurant. Police are on their way now to arrest you for public urination. I could go on...

Today we are witness to an early generation of device called a biometric scanner. This device captures a picture of your face and compares it to other faces in its database. If your features resemble those of a known criminal or terrorist whose face is in the database, you will likely be detained. Some people speculate that if you look too much like someone else, authorities might actually believe you are that person. I suppose it's possible and a SWAT team could be called and you could be accidentally shot in the confusion. Chances are, though, that if you're not the actual terrorist or criminal in the database, the worst that you'll suffer is just more inconvenience and embarrassment.

For the moment, I'm not too concerned. As long as this kind of technology is only employed in public arenas and is utilized solely to maintain safety and security, I'm not worried. The worst that would likely happen is some security guard might see me pick my nose, scratch my crotch, or stare down the shirt of some hottie. However, if the government starts moving further down the road of blanket phone taps and broader domestic spying powers (all in the name of rooting out terrorism, of course), we may as well move to China.

Some civil libertarians see any move by the government to better monitor the public as a slippery slope into an abyss of fascism. I generally don't buy into "slippery slope" arguments. I usually believe that there's always some middle ground on any issue. But while protests from civil libertarians are going largely unheeded these days (after all, when people are frightened, the instinct to survive supercedes the desire for freedom), I think we should all bear in mind Patrick Henry's famous rallying cry, "Give me liberty or give me death!" This should be our mantra (albeit a tad extreme) through this crisis. We must be vigilant against abuses of our civil rights. Otherwise, measures enacted to protect us from terror will accomplish exactly what our enemies want.

Biometric Scanning & Civil Rights, Part III

Joseph G. Carson   December 10, 2001

U ntil now, I had been convinced that the September 11th attacks were masterminded by none other than Representative Gary Condit (I mean, most people these days would say "Chandra who?"). But as time goes on, I'm beginning to think that the whole thing was instigated by high-tech security companies. I mean, the use of biometrics at the Superbowl two years ago caused a huge furor, and Florida's use of "faceprinting" technology at traffic lights provoked enough outcry that the practice was discontinued. All this is due to change, it seems, and despite the hand-wringing by the Cassandras of Big Brotherhood, I cannot imagine that there will be enough public outcry to overcome the tide of paranoid fear that seems to have swept the country. No one wants to board an airplane and find themselves flying into a tall building a couple of hours later. In my opinion, air travel is horrid enough as it is – airports full of long lines and strikingly unhelpful personnel, the stomach-churning take-offs and landings. One gets used to it, people tell me, but one also gets used to gang sodomy after enough time in prison. I've always opted for the train.

And now, with the addition of biometric scans in airports such as LAX (and being considered at many major terminals across the country), I feel like I have another reason to disdain air travel. I am a (mostly) law-abiding citizen without even a traffic violation to my name, but I am troubled by the idea that soon databases will be swelling with info about my whereabouts. The idea must be that if I were a violent terrorist, I would be apprehended, but how is that information known beforehand? Because I visit web sites that are supportive of Palestinian causes, for instance? Because I don't support the bombing campaign? Because I watch *Politically Incorrect*?

Moreover, how are we supposed to be assured of the reliability of this technology? Much like the missile defense shield, we're only told how it's supposed to work, but not how it actually parses the ones and zeroes to make us all safe from terrorism. How many accidental detainments will take place? How many people (probably of Middle Eastern descent) will not be allowed to board a plane because their cheek bone-to-lip-to-forehead ratio is too close to someone who once wrote an article critical of America's Middle East policies?

Trying to do research, one finds that there isn't much publicly available about the new use of biometrics. I say "new" to distinguish these uses of biometrics from its traditional use, which has been with us since the early part of the 20th century. Biometrics, at its most basic, is simply the numerical analysis of data ("metrics") derived from the life sciences ("bio"). Thus, a study analyzing the efficacy of various treatments for a particular disease to determine the most useful is an example of old-school biometrics.

This new use of the term, in fact, the traditional biometricists seek to disassociate themselves from. The Journal of Biometrics now sports a disclaimer on its web site stating that they know nothing about this use of biometrics and could people please stop calling them. I don't blame them; I'm sure their phone has been ringing off the hook, since they're pretty much the only presence one can find on the issue. I imagine that, much like missile defense and INS detentions, we're simply not told much about the details, you know, for our protection.

And so what can anyone say about it? It will happen; this use of biometrics will increasingly become a part of our lives, and I imagine soon such technology will be employed at grocery stores, at traffic lights, movie theatres... I can't imagine that within 20 years we won't have an infrastructure in place to track pretty much every person any place they care to go. In the wake of September 11th, at least for the foreseeable future, who is going to stand up to these changes? Any outcry of protest is going to be met with the inevitable "If you don't have anything to hide, there's no reason for you to be concerned about this." And that's going to shut a lot of people up. The liberal press has been largely supportive of any and all measures which *might* (the operative word) decrease the likelihood of a terrorist attack. And so we will continue to watch as technology encroaches upon our freedom in the name of preserving it. Thus, in the wake of September 11th, the pendulum swings hard in the direction of more surveillance, more paranoia, more technology seeking to protect us from a nebulous evil Other. The question is whether the pendulum will ever swing back.

Osama, You No-Tipping Whore

Chad Schnaible   February 24, 2002

Recently (and apparently because of this recession) the nincompoopity of the Bush administration, and my love for the American musical, I've had to find a new job. What job, you ask, could this college-educated man with decent acting and writing skills find? You guessed it: a pizza delivery driver.

Now, for reasons of corporate and national security, I cannot use the store's real name, so I'll refer to it by a pseudonym: Pizza Smut. So, I got a job at Pizza Smut, working nights, running red lights, and virtually running my mini-van into the ground. Oh, the joys of working food service in small-town Mississippi! What follows is a general account of events and wacky shenanigans that occur during a regular 5-10 shift:

4:55 p.m.

Our hero (me) arrives at work. No other night-shift employees have arrived, since it's seems to be some kind of unwritten rule that you shouldn't show up until 10 minutes after you're supposed to be at work.

5:05 p.m.

Four deliveries are ready to go all at the same time. Where's the other driver? That's the kicker. There is no other driver. Because this is a weeknight, our manager decides it couldn't possibly be busy enough to warrant the $18 needed to pay another driver for three hours work. He almost always overlooks our nation's ever-growing addiction to greasy, artery-clogging nourishment.

5:45 p.m.

After making four deliveries in record time, our hero returns to the store with a pocketful of change from the Guy Who-Always-Pays-With-Fucking-Quarters. Now, there are six deliveries up, most of which are at 45 minutes after the time the customer called (Pizza Smut policy ordains that deliveries should leave the store within 20 minutes of the customer's call).

39

6:12 p.m.

Our hero is lost in the boonies. Mississippi has apparently never heard of city planning. Every street has a name; few have numbers. Most houses have no numbers on them. There is no grid. The map is nothing more than a random spray of sub-divisions laid down without rhyme nor reason, named Cotton Patch, Quail Grove, Tara Estates, and other nauseating rustic, rural appellations.

6:22 p.m.

Our hero finds a gas station and a pay phone. The customer is mystified that he couldn't find the apartment. The customer is sure "off of Molly Bar on Old Highway 7" should have been "plenty good" directions, and this driver must be "special." This driver bites his tongue and refrains from telling the customer he's a complete ignoramus and might as well be living on Mars, his dwelling was so easy to locate.

6:50 p.m.

Our hero returns to the store, finding most deliveries at an hour. Upon checking the computer, he finds there are several deliveries entered that he has no slips for. He contemplates suicide first, then mass-murder. Maybe he should just quit. He decides he'd rather not go to the Mississippi State Penitentiary, and he really needs some cash. He grabs four more deliveries and sprints out the door.

7:02 p.m.

A man living in abject squalor gives our hero a hard time because it's been a whole 45 minutes since he's placed his order. Our hero thinks he should be so lucky. It could've been 90 minutes. The man reluctantly pays and asks for his 75 cents in change. Our hero looks at him as if he's joking, then explains he doesn't carry loose change. The man doesn't seem to hear him. The man proceeds to scrape together 25 cents from his couch cushions and asks for a dollar back. Our hero makes a note to himself to wash his hands at least three times after handling sticky change.

7:32 p.m.

Our hero returns to the store. He is asked by the servers to please answer the phone, which is ringing on all five lines. Our hero giggles, mutters something incoherently, grabs four more deliveries, and leaves.

8:05 p.m.

Our hero returns again after making four deliveries on campus without any tips. College students have a general consensus that since they are poor, this allows them to be cheap as well.

8:10 p.m. - 10:00 p.m.

Reread events above. They repeat themselves nearly word for word.

10:00 p.m. - midnight

Our hero is stuck doing "prep work," which means the day crew is too damn lazy to get their shit ready. He races about the store, wondering if there is such a thing as a health code in Mississippi, since a dark-brown crud occupies every corner and crack of this restaurant. He finally leaves, dazed, confused, and thoroughly irritated.

This is just a sample of the torture which I undergo. Not that you care. You all have cushy jobs where you sit on your asses all day sipping half-caff lattes with twists of lemon. All I've got to say to you is, "Can you get me a job there?"

I guess I should blame the whole mess on Osama Bin Laden. Why not? This "war on terrorism" seems to have frozen the economy. Nobody wants to spend their money. Huge corporations like Enron and K-Mart are folding. Maybe I should go into Stealth Bomber manufacturing or war bonds. You know, go where the money is. I just want Osama to know that if I ever have to deliver a pizza to his cave, he better give me damn good directions or it's going to be late. Really late. And I expect a tip.

I'm constantly amazed at our outright ignorance of (or disdain for) other countries and cultures. I don't think this is a uniquely American trait (I hope not), but I do think we are probably leaders in the "there's a world outside our borders?" race. I'm no world scholar, and no one would ever call me well-travelled (Jeremy is the only one of us who truly deserves to be called that), but, seriously, folks, would it hurt you to listen to the BBC news once in a while?

A Geo-Political Primer

David Nett   March 4, 2002

A week or so ago, my good friend Jeremy sent an email to all of us Clark Schpiellians about the reported death of a guerilla leader in Angola, and the implications for possible peace in the region after long years of civil war. On the same day, I read a comment from Natalie Jeremijenko, an engineering professor at Yale (in an article in *Salon.com* about robotic reporters in foreign conflicts), which stated, "...for most Americans, Afghanistan might as well be Mars." My reaction to both of these comments was, "there are other countries?"

After some lengthy internet investigation, I was able to discover that there are indeed several countries outside of the United States – these places often have their own laws and languages (though they still watch American television and movies – no one on earth can miss "Must See TV"). From what I could tell, there may be as many as 10 or 15 of these "other countries." In fact, two of them, "Canada" and "Mexico," share portions of our continent!

I've put together a quick primer, based entirely upon un-substantiated information from the internet and the walls of a bathroom stall in the DuPar's on Sunset Blvd., comparing our dear United States with Canada, Mexico and "Other Countries," in a variety of important areas. After reading this, you'll be able to speak with confidence about international issues at keggers, gallery-openings, and State of the Union Addresses (we know you are reading, GWB ;-). This is just one small example of *CSP*'s continuing dedication to the intellectual growth of our dear troglodytic readers.

System of Government

United States	The United States is a representative democracy, where electorates, representing a geographical grouping of the population and informed by a general election, vote for elected officials. Checks and balances keep any one official from gaining too much power.

Canada	Canada, our "neighbor to the north", is ruled through a joint arrangement by a delegation of displaced, dirty Frenchmen and exiled British ex-patriots, whose decisions are balanced by a single Polar Bear with a magic 8-ball.
Mexico	In Mexico, each town is governed in a totalitarian manner by a local bandit (or, "bandito") king, often referred to as "Jefe," who encourages his tequila-fueled followers to ride through town, shooting their pistolas into the air.
Other Countries	Each country is ruled through an agreement between a local military or religious dictator, and either the U.S. President or Bill Gates.

Predominant Transportation

United States	Nearly every person owns an automobile which costs only slightly more than a citizen of any other country will earn in his or her lifetime, and they are driven on a complex network of streets and highways.
Canada	For downhill trips, Canadians rely upon bobsleds or luges. Uphill trips: ski-lifts.
Mexico	For short trips, Mexicans walk or ride burros. For longer trips, a Mexican will eat anywhere from 3 to 10 carefully crafted Hot Tamales, after which his/her eyes will bug out, steam will explode from his/her ears, and he/she will be rocketed across the arid countryside toward his/her destination with flames shooting out of his/her ass.
Other Countries	Camels. Occasionally, elephants or dragons.

Currency

United States	The Dollar is the base unit of currency, and is broken down into coins of various denominations.
Canada	In order to avoid confusion during gambling trips to the United States, Canada also wisely uses the Dollar. Unfortunately unable to print their own money (cold weather freezes the ink), they are forced to use Monopoly money.

Mexico	Burritos, Enchiladas and Beef Mexi-Melts. 7 Burritos to an Enchilada, 4.5 Enchiladas to a Beef Mexi-Melt. The value of the Burrito base, in US Dollars, can be found at any local Taco Bell.
Other Countries	Dollars, Burritos, little pieces of colored plastic -- whatever the United States gives them.

Chief Exports

United States	Pride, Freedom, Frivolous Litigation.
Canada	Snowmen, Hockey Players, Michael J. Fox.
Mexico	Tequila, Sombreros.
Other Countries	Drugs, inexpensive automobiles, and skanky, no talent actresses.

National Symbols

United States	The majestic bald eagle.
Canada	Maple Leaf & Michael J. Fox.
Mexico	Quetzalcoatl, the feathered serpent-god, and "Tuko" from the Good, the Bad and the Ugly (oddly, actually played by Eli Wallach, who is not Mexican).
Other Countries	A hammer, a star, a sickle and Mr. Bean, in various configurations.

Attitudes Toward the United States

United States	We fucking love us! We think we kick ass!
Canada	Although they greatly dislike being referred to as "the 51st State," they love to see the familiar Toronto or Vancouver skylines in so many of our syndicated television shows.
Mexico	Mexico has a love-hate relationship with the US: They hate that we shoot them when they try to run across our border, but they love that we are perfectly happy to purchase their narcotics at ridiculous prices and shoot them up our smug, self-righteous asses.
Other Countries	Who gives two shits?

After 9/11 and the subsequent (and justified) invasion of Afghanistan, I began to feel an increasing trepidation about the George W. Bush administration. I started to feel that maybe he wasn't so funny, so clownish, but rather that his faux-populism concealed something, well, a little sinister. But I wasn't sure of what to do about it, or how to really express my fears. Obviously, I didn't feel president Bush was evil, or deliberately trying to sabotage America (I still don't), but more and more it became apparent that his administration represented a rejection of almost everything for which I stood, and embraced an embarassingly simplistic "us vs. them" world view, wherein the way we conducted ourselves as a nation was far less important than our somehow "winning" the war against evil.

This realization scared the crap outta me.

Civil Liberty vs. Bush's War on Terror

David Nett   June 24, 2002

So, two weeks ago, we all learned that U.S. officials captured a dude, nearly a month ago, who was planning to attack the U.S. with a "dirty nuke." He was born Jose Padilla, and now is called Abdullah al-Muhajir. He grew up in Chicago, and U.S. officials say he was a gang member as a teen, though Chicago police say there is no hard evidence at this time to support this statement. U.S. officials say he was trained by Al Qaeda in Afghanistan and possibly Pakistan not only to be a terrorist, but to build explosives. He also, they say, probably studied information about radioactivity. They say, though there has yet to be disclosed any proof that a plan was ever begun, much less carried out, and no evidence of any explosives or equipment to build explosives was found, that he was part of a potential plot to destroy our way of life. So, even though he is a U.S. citizen, and was not captured in any illicit illegal act or committing any violent crime against U.S. citizens or soldiers, the Bush administration has declared him an "Enemy Combatant" which, under Bush's November 19th declaration, allows us to hold him indefinitely, without benefit of a lawyer, without charging him of any crime, and without any of the guaranteed protections offered to U.S. citizens by the Constitution, or to Prisoners of War by the Geneva Convention.

Okay – my paranoia about the actions of the Bush administration, especially during this ongoing "War on Terror," can be traced to many different sources. It may be that I watched Oliver Stone's *Salvador* last weekend. It may also be that, two days later, I watched the 4-hour HBO movie, *Fidel*. It may be that I struggle with the kind of illogical knee-jerk liberal sensibilities that really only come from rebelling against a relatively comfortable middle-class life with conservative parents. It may be that, during my teen years, I believed fanatically in the ideals of the Reagan government, my conservative parents, my grandfather (a Republican state representative), and Rush Limbaugh, and am now horrified by those memories. It may also be that I'm trying to atone for that one afternoon during my junior year of high school when I told my hippie physics teacher,

Mr. Schmid, that liberals were all fucking stupid, and that Ronald Reagan should be the fifth face on Mount Rushmore. That comment will give me nightmares for the rest of my adult life.

But, whatever the cause of my general suspicion over the motives of George Bush and his cronies, my thoughts about this case in particular can be traced to the following facts:

1. Jose Padilla is a U.S. citizen.

2. U.S. law affords all U.S. citizens, no matter what their suspected crime, certain rights.

3. In declaring him an enemy combatant, Padilla is denied all of the rights granted him by U.S. law, including the right to legal counsel, and the right to be charged with a crime within a reasonable amount of time.

4. Accused criminals like John Walker Lindh (the guy who was captured fighting with the Taliban just a few weeks into our incursion into Afghanistan) and Richard Reid (the guy who tried to blow up a plane using a homemade shoe-bomb) are being afforded their legal rights to trial and representation.

What these facts say to me is this: unlike in the Lindh or Reid cases, the government does not have enough evidence on Padilla to actually formally accuse him of a crime and have it stick. Lindh and Reid allegedly made plans whose nature was similar to those of which Padilla is accused, both at least attempted to carry them out, and there appears to be much evidence against them. Padilla, so far as we know, never got so far as to even formally plan his supposed attack on the U.S., and the evidence against him (what we've heard of it, anyway) seems largely circumstantial. So, since the government's evidence is sketchy, it declares Padilla an enemy combatant so he can be held indefinitely, without access to legal counsel, while the government builds its case. Further supporting this notion is the fact that, under the rules Bush declared last year for enemy combatants, military tribunals, and the like, Padilla, a U.S. citizen, cannot be tried by military tribunal. So, he sits in military hands only until the federal government has sufficient hard evidence to formally accuse him of something, or until the "War on Terrorism" is over. Or, forever – whichever comes first.

For all my ranting, it is possible, maybe even probable, that Padilla is a terrorist, or, at least, a wanna-be terrorist. The media, so far, has painted a pretty convincing picture of his guilt. He has certainly had a history of crime (albeit mostly petty) here in the U.S., and it appears he did spend time in Pakistan and elsewhere in the middle east, possibly under the tutelage of other suspected terrorists. He could well be a dangerous terrorist, harboring the secrets of a deadly plot. But that doesn't mean we can break the law in an attempt to stop him. The U.S. Constitution grants certain rights to all U.S. citizens, especially those accused of crimes, so that they may defend themselves against false accusation. When we remove those rights, even for those accused of the most despicable and unthinkable crimes, we narrow the gap between ourselves and those who want to destroy our way of life. The United States of America is, or at least is supposed to be, a country of freedoms, of civil liberties, as well as laws which protect its people. We gasped in terror when we heard about women, accused of petty crimes without evidence, publicly executed in the Taliban's Afghanistan. While I don't mean to say that the suspension of Padilla's legal rights is akin to that horror, it is a step toward injustice, rather than a step away.

All of this goes not only for Padilla, but for all prisoners, accused criminals, and innocent bystanders who are purposefully or unintentionally harmed by our new "War on Terror." We must approach our new enemies (or, "evildoers" as the simpleton in the White House explains to us) with the same respect and recognition of the law which we would afford to any other human being. It is not enough to *say* that we are the land of the free, we must *act* that way. The accused are innocent until proven guilty, even those accused of terrorism. Human life is precious, including the lives of radical Islamic extremists, despite what angry rednecks may fold into the lyrics of country music. The more we kill and destroy those who hate us without trying to root out the cause of that hate in our own policies and practices, the more we are hated. There's a reason we are despised throughout the world (even by some of our own allies), and suspending the rights of our own citizens because they are accused of a crime does not help matters.

And remember (this may not be a popular stance, but I'm gonna go for it), we were once terrorists, too. Granted, our grand act was throwing a bunch of tea into the harbor, but we also raided armories and engaged in guerilla warfare. It's hardly the same thing as killing thousands of innocent civilians to promote terror, I know, but my point is that we fought our guerilla war so that it would be legally recognized that all men are created equal, and are entitled to all of the protections afforded under the law. If we circumvent these rights, even for accused terrorists, how can we say we are any better than our historical oppressors, or even those "terrorists" we now fight against? Being a patriot, I imagine, is about believing strongly in, and fighting for, the constitution, the liberties, the freedoms, and the laws of the country to which you are loyal. And that means all of the laws, for all of the people, all of the time. Anything less is hypocrisy.

The GWB cartoons came about because I couldn't figure out how to write an essay combining the Enron crash and Bush's alarming "faith-based initiatives." Plus, big heads on little bodies always equals funny.

GWB Luvs God

David Nett   July 15, 2002

And I say again that we should not fear religion, and that federal money used to support faith-based programs will not be used to evang ... evangel ... promote religion, but rather to help communities.

After all, in these troubled economic times (which, incidently, I inherited and have not exac ... exacer ... made worse in any way with grossly inappropriate tax cuts which favor, in many cases, the very rich over the poor and middle classes), who better to accept our money than God? In fact, I've known Him for years – He's a close personal friend, and I've had several meetings with Him, at the White House and elsewhere.

Heaven has just announced they overstated $6 billion in revenues in 1999. 70% of the Celestial Choir will be laid off in the next week, and God has stepped down as CEO. So, ix-nay on the aith-fay.

Um ... so, how 'bout them Evildoers?

Bush Declares Gore Enemy Combatant

David Nett   July 29, 2002

In a shrewd and startling move at a press conference yesterday, President George W. Bush declared former Vice President Al Gore, his opponent in the 2000 presidential elections, an Enemy Combatant.

"He [Gore], with his criticisms of the current 'Holy War on Terror,' is a clear and present threat to all that we as Americans hold dear, and an out-and-out Evildoer of the first degree" declared the President from the Whitehouse steps late Sunday evening. "However," Bush continued, "since Gore has done nothing technically illegal, I am forced to use the powers granted to me by me during this dire time of not-legally-declared war to declare him an 'Enemy Combatant,' so that I can have him locked up in a military prison until our all-important War Against the Evildoers ends, or forever, whichever comes first."

When asked what prompted this startling, unprecedented move, the President seemed very comfortable and casual. "I've got nothing against Al personally," President Bush replied, "but he's been speaking out a lot lately about this and that, and questioning my politics in an ex ... extre ... very not-patriotic manner. Then, yesterday morning I was on the phone with Dad and uncle Ron and we were talking about how we had to crack down on and wipe out all of the Godless Communists – I mean, Saddam's factions – I mean, Anti-American Evildoers, and that anyone who opposed our Holy Crusade must be silenced. And then I thought, 'that Gore guy has been saying the stuff I do is bad. I'll start with him.'"

The President also volunteered more information about other possible "enemy combatants." "Sometimes I stay up late on Saturdays, and on that *Saturday Night Live* show, they sometimes make fun of me and of our Great Crusade," the President offered. "So, watch out, Will Ferrell and Tina Fey. There's a windowless cell in an undisclosed military installation with your names on it." The president then added, "but that Jimmy Fallon can rest easy. He's just too damn cute to incarcerate indefinitely under inhumane conditions without benefit of legal counsel or even formal charges."

When pressed for more, President Bush politely declined to comment, saying he had to get back to the business of distracting the media from the desperately floundering US economy, continuing revelations over underhanded corporate accounting, his own administration's history of allegedly shady business dealings, a desperate Afghan interim government (and revelations of ongoing excessive US force in that region), by announcing plans to overthrow Saddam Hussein's Iraqi government and, "if that don't do the job, possibly France. They're a royal pain in the rear."

Al Gore was unable to comment on the surprise action, as he is being held by the US Armed Forces, possibly in an undisclosed military prison, and is not being allowed any contact with friends, family, lawyers, or the media. Military officials assured us, however, that he would be released as soon as the War on Terror was over. Probably.

Jimmy Fallon and Tina Fey were similarly indisposed in a secluded lower east-side holding cell, where Lorne Michaels reportedly keeps the *SNL* cast locked away during the summer hiatus. Will Ferrell, having recently escaped from such a facility, was still too bewildered to give an interview.

GWB: Cowboy

David Nett   August 5, 2002

People of America and the World: tonight I wish to inform you that we intend to invade Iraq, and topple the ruthless, anti-Christian government of Saddam Hussein. You may remember Saddam from the war which made my daddy briefly popular. Well, this time the Bush popularity won't be so fleeting — Saddam's gonna git Sad-*bombed*, if you git my drift.

Iraq has refused weapons inspectors & laughed at sanctions, & its people are not Christians, & hate us & God. Covered women & unkempt facial hair, & Saddam's mustache, haunt my dreams. Who knows when they will rise up & attack our way of life? Better we launch a pre..pre-em..pre..strike before they do, wipe out the government, replace it with an unstable interim government which can't succeed, & then move on to fight another nation before we really assist in rebuilding the country whose current government (which, again, we are gonna whup-up on) we helped to build in the first place. It's just the right thing to do.

Psst. The United Nations and a coalition of countries, including many of our closest allies, plus Russia and China, have condemned the idea of attacking Iraq without direct proof of a demonstrated wrong-doing or real threat by the Iraqi government. They agree that Saddam is a tyrant, but have said have said they cannot and will not support an unprovoked US attack.

Yee-Haw! I'm a Cowboy!

When, a year after the 9/11 tragedy, with our troops still deeply engaged in Afghanistan, it began to look like Bush and company were marching toward a second war in Iraq, I was incredulous. Mind you, I believed Sadaam had, or was trying to get, Weapons of Mass Destruction. Most of us did – not having an intelligence branch here at CSP, we were forced to take the words of George Tenet's CIA and the Department of Defense's intelligence analysts. Still, a second war in one year, this one with no provocation – surely GWB was just bluffing. Right?

For the record: he was not.

One Year Gone

David Nett   September 10, 2002

The guy who sits in the cube next to me at work doesn't get a birthday this year. Or any year hereafter, presumably. You see, this fellow (we'll call him "Mark," mostly 'cause his name is "Mark") has the newly unfortunate birth date of September 11, 1974. I'm guessing he didn't have much of a party last year, and he'll certainly not have much of a party this year. In fact, he'll be in danger of revealing a traitorous hatred for our country if he even cracks a smile on his 28th birthday. I find this supremely sad, not only because Mark deserves to celebrate his fucking birthday if he wants to, but because this is perhaps the most significant way in which my "world has been changed forever" in the past year.

Right upfront, I just want to say that I mean in no way to belittle the terrible loss felt by those who lost friends and relatives in the terrorist attack of last year, or who lost businesses and livelihoods in the wake of the tragedy. For those people, life has certainly been forever horribly altered. And my heart goes out to all of those folks. But for the rest of us, what difference has the second-most (or most, depending upon how you feel about Pearl Harbor) dramatic attack by a foreign power on U.S. soil really made? Has our world view opened up? Have we looked with compassion or a desire for understanding at the rest of the world? In a word, "nope."

I'm gonna go all mushy-leftist here. In an essay I wrote days after the attacks last year, I implored our government (assuming, of course, that among the handful of unique folks who visit our site each week, there were several extremely high-ranking government officials) to act with restraint, to value liberty and justice over revenge, and to call upon the basic human compassion of the people of the world, rather than calling out the dogs of war. I think it's obvious to most that our government did not listen to me (note to self: add GWB to the CSP mailing list). What we got instead was a suppression of civil liberty, a gathering of unprecedented Executive power in the hands of our barely-elected president, and such a sense of self-righteousness and frontier lynch-mobism (my new word – you heard it first here), that all but our very closest ally (Great Britain) have become alarmed and disgusted with us. In short, instead of 9/11 waking us up to our place in this new, very small world, and forcing us to try to understand, and hopefully begin to reverse, the hatred of the U.S. that consumes a great part of this globe, we've acted so fiercely and unilaterally, without even a care for what the rest of the world community thinks, that even our friends have begun to hate us.

And, now that all the world (except Great Britain) is desperately trying to talk GWB out of bombing the bejeezus out of Iraq, we pause to remember what, in our minds, started this all: the acts of terrorism that killed 3000 people and brought our country, at least temporarily, to its knees. Except, 9/11 isn't what started it, whatever we may want to think. And that's the problem. Twenty-four hours of non-stop sensationalist reporting about what really happened 9/11/01, with pictures of the burning towers and Pentagon flashed onscreen every three seconds, and weepy interviews with the deservedly heartbroken family members of the victims, will only serve to re-ignite our anger, and the point will, once again, be entirely missed.

And the point is this: we're fucking it up. Everyday the world is a smaller place. We (the U.S.) are a huge fish in an increasingly shrinking pond. We're eating more than we need, we're shitting more than any fish deserves to. We're thrashing about as we please, without regard for the smaller fish who could and do get hurt with every nonchalant flick of our tail. And we've got to stop. We have a responsibility as human beings to at least try to understand the needs, the wants, the desires and the freedoms of every human being on this planet, and to consider those needs whenever we take any action, inside or outside our borders. We have to stop assuming our wishes and desires are mirrored by the rest of the world. We have to stop assuming that everyone who disagrees with us is wrong. We have to listen. We have to act in concert with our allies, and our increasingly important global institutions (such as the U.N.). We have to put human rights and civil liberties before paranoia and revenge fantasies, and before corporate profits and trade relations. We'll never please everyone and, simply because we are big and powerful, we'll always be hated by someone. But we have to learn compassion, and show our love of liberty and freedom and law and due-process by offering that liberty and freedom and law and due-process to everyone. And, what's more, we have to learn not to be offended if not everyone wants to accept our offerings. Not everyone agrees with us. And that's good, because often we are not right.

Because the reality is this: if we do not start to clean up our act on an international scale, this is only gonna get worse. There are lots of people out there who, for a wide range of often very legitimate reasons, hate us. And every time we reach out and squash one of them without the support of the international community, even if we fear they might be and (probably are) plotting against us, the rest hate us even more, and one or two who were on the fence fall into that "hate us" bucket. And, because we're big and powerful and scary, most of those folks feel the only way to hurt us is by terrorizing our people. For them, 9/11 was only the beginning.

So, as we sit in front of the television tomorrow, teary-eyed and pointedly not celebrating my buddy Mark's birthday, let's pause to consider what the rest of the world is thinking as they watch. GWB may not agree, but it's high time we start to care about what the world thinks. There are worse things than what happened to us a year ago. All over the world, people live with those "worse things" every day. We need to try to understand. If we don't, the hate just continues.

Another Iraqi War?

Jeremy Groce   November 4, 2002

S hould we go to war against Iraq? This question is currently dominating conversations around the country, especially among our political leaders in Washington, D.C. As usual, there are those on both sides of the issue who believe that the answer is simple. The answer, of course, is not simple. In fact, I believe we cannot answer the question at all unless we ponder several questions that have not yet been asked and consider an alternative framework for improving the U.S.-Iraq relationship.

Assuming we believe what our government says and what we read in the news, Saddam Hussein has chemical weapons and likely has biological weapons. By all accounts, he is also working to build (or acquire) nuclear weapons. The Bush administration, and many other Americans, believe that Saddam Hussein cannot be trusted with any weapons of mass destruction because his hatred of the U.S. will spur him to use one of these weapons against the U.S. (or an ally like Turkey or Israel), or provide such weapons to a terrorist organization. These "hawks" want to pre-emptively strike Iraq militarily and eliminate Saddam. Some hawks (and a majority of Americans, according to some polls) believe we should attack only with the support and assistance of our allies and the United Nations, but most hawks in the administration believe that an attack must be made as soon as possible, regardless of other nations' decisions.

For a variety of reasons, many Americans oppose the idea of attacking Iraq. These "doves" believe that an attack against Iraq would be wrong. Some believe that an attack should not be made unless clear and unequivocal proof exists that Saddam intends to attack us or an ally, or that he has or is on the verge of having, nuclear weapons. In short, they wonder, why must we attack now? What's the rush? Isn't Saddam still several years away from nuclear capabilities? Others believe that we must concentrate solely on diplomatic means to eliminate Saddam's weapons or weapons programs. Let weapons inspectors go in and do their jobs and keep us abreast of developments, they argue.

Recent occurrences in North Korea reveal the potential problems with this line of thinking. Jimmy Carter was just awarded a Nobel Peace Prize, in part due to his efforts in negotiating a non-proliferation agreement with North Korea under Kim Il Sung. Now that same nation, under Kim Jong Il, has announced that they possess nuclear weapons and has implied that the world must now meet to discuss other demands … or else. Clearly the agreements they made with Carter were nothing more than bids to buy time. How can we be sure that Saddam will not do the same? And if he permits weapons inspectors back into Iraq, what should our response be if (when) he obfuscates their efforts?

Some doves argue that an attack against Iraq is wrong simply because there are more important things for our government to be concerned about, like the U.S. economy, jobs, and healthcare. While I believe these other issues are legitimate concerns, I would argue that these doves miss the big picture. Surely the possibility that a homicidal dictator like Saddam Hussein could attack us with nuclear weapons should take precedence.

Many doves oppose the Bush administration's oft-stated goal of "regime change," arguing that we can't simply topple every leader we don't like. I certainly agree, though Saddam's clear willingness to use weapons of mass destruction and his extreme hatred of the United States place him in a unique category. Also, given Saddam's apparent intransience on the issue of disarmament, it is likely that only a regime change in Iraq would result in any lasting change of relations.

There is a similar dove argument that says we shouldn't attack Iraq simply for possessing weapons of mass destruction. After all, plenty of other countries have weapons of mass destruction and we're not planning to invade them. Again, this is true, but at the present we have no fear that France, India, China, or any of the other nuclear powers are likely to use these weapons against us.

As you can see, I can argue against opposition to an attack on Iraq. This is not the same, however, as arguing for an attack on Iraq. I think there are several key questions that must first be answered – if they can be – if we are to feel confident that any decision we make on this issue is right.

1. What kind of war must we fight to disarm Saddam? If it is a large-scale conflict like the 1991 Gulf War, the U.S. will need to spend huge sums of money. If our armed forces enter Iraq and make a real effort to capture

or kill Saddam, the human sacrifices may also be extensive. Should the United States focus our resources on a war that may or may not make us safe? Do we sacrifice, say, 10,000 US soldiers in a war to topple Saddam in order to save the lives of 3,000 civilians who might be killed in a potential terror attack committed by Saddam's regime or a Saddam-supported terrorist cell? What risks are we willing to accept for potential gains? In other words, do we know that inaction will have greater consequences than action?

2. What should the United States' policy be towards nations that choose to develop weapons of mass destruction? What if they are purely defensive weapons? After all, it has been argued that Saddam is simply accumulating weapons of mass destruction as an insurance policy, designed to keep him and his chosen successors in power for as long as he (and they) like, without interference from rebel or foreign armies. Saddam may not be so diabolical as to use such weapons against the U.S. or an ally. I would also argue that he might not risk letting such weapons fall into the hands of Islamic fundamentalist terrorist groups for fear that these groups may use these weapons against him and his secular regime.

3. What are the dangers of a general pre-emptive strike policy? What kind of message do we send the rest of the world, particularly countries like Israel, China, and Russia, who have their own reasons for wanting to invade or attack neighbors?

4. Do we have a concrete plan for reconstructing Iraq and are we prepared to carry out the plan, regardless of the time and money it may require?

5. Here's a question no one asks: are American lives more valuable than Iraqi lives? Is it acceptable to Americans that thousands of Iraqi soldiers and civilians die in our fight to protect American lives from possible attack (I highlight the word "possible," because I think it is virtually universally accepted that if we were certain of an attack or imminent attack on the United States by Iraq, Americans would by and large support whatever actions necessary to eliminate the threat)?

6. What are some other possible unintended disasters that could result from an attack on Iraq? Might it lead to other nations and peoples hating American hegemony and power? If we topple Saddam and his regime and U.S.-led efforts to reconstruct the nation fail, what happens to the

balance of power and relative stability in the Middle East?

7. What happens if the U.S. does not attack Iraq and a year from now we or an ally is attacked and it is revealed that Saddam Hussein and Iraq were involved?

At the moment, I can't answer these questions. So for now, I favor the following:

1. Offer Saddam positive reinforcement. Say that if weapons inspectors are offered unfettered access to any site at any time throughout the country, the West will gradually lift economic sanctions. Any impediment of inspections will result in a return of sanctions and (possibly) limited strikes against military targets.

2. Indirectly support the Iraqi people's efforts to change the regime from within. Promote democracy and improvement of human rights conditions within Iraq the way we do in China – by advancing the causes of free markets, access to education, and economic liberalism. Work with NGOs and the Iraqi government to create an environment wherein Saddam would gain nothing by destabilizing the region or attacking the West.

3. Make it 100 percent clear to Saddam clear that any attack against the US or its allies, by his regime or any terrorist organization that can be linked to him and his regime, will be seen as an act of war and will provoke an appropriate response.

If Saddam resists these changes, persists in efforts to create arsenals of devastating weapons, or directly or indirectly attacks the U.S. or our allies, then a U.S. military response may be required.

Other Homeland Security Additions

David Nett   November 25, 2002

Last Tuesday, the Senate passed the long-debated Homeland Security Bill, despite grave misgivings about some of the bill's late-in-life additions, including provisions which allow the government to contract with companies who've moved off-shore to avoid taxes, protect pharmaceutical companies (retroactively, even) from being liable for vaccine side-effects, and establish a security research lab facility in Bush's state of Texas, on the Texas A&M campus. While those provisions are the most debated, other not-quite-kosher provisions managed to slip under the media's radar:

- Provision 127.27.a, which states that all Americans must hereafter refer to Trent Lott as "Daddy."

- Provision 77.1c, which lists the 10 hottest TV heartthrobs of all time, wherein Bea Arthur edges out Heather Locklear for the top spot.

- Provision 444a, which renames all of the Midwest (including Oklahoma, Nebraska, Iowa, Minnesota, and North and South Dakotas) "North Texas," and California "Dirty Hippie-ville."

- Provision 116.36.g, which states that "Solar Power" and "Alternative Fuel Sources" will be referred to as "Commie Power" and "Anti-American Fuel Sources," respectively.

- Provision 3.f, which replaces the 3 remaining liberals on Capitol Hill with Joe "I'm almost a Republican" Lieberman clones.

- Provision 67.99.21.k, which declares Osama Bin Laden dead already, so we can commence with the bombing of somebody else.

- Provision 69.b, which deals with the abolition of non-executive wages in American corporations. Workers must continue to come to work, but they will no longer be paid. Instead, they must make a "purchase request" to the company's finance dept. for each item they wish to buy, including all clothing, food items and medicines. If approved, items will be requisitioned and employees may pick them up on the third Sunday of each month. Water will, according to a separate paragraph, be distributed freely by the cupful, after work hours. Employees must supply their own cups, which can be purchased via "Water Cup Requisition Form 1145z." Executives will continue to be paid at current salary inflation rates.

- Provision 888c, which allows corporations to run for political office, effectively cutting out the middle-man. Vote for Pespi/Microsoft in 2004!

My Outrage

David Nett   February 24, 2003

I'm not a particularly angry person. Unlike my lesbian friend Jeanette, who
has killed seven men (that we know of) for asking to touch her boobs, or
fellow *Clark Schpiell* founder Dr. M, who once twisted Jeremy's head off (it
was promptly re-attached by Dr. Epstein, the father of our only childhood
Jewish friend), I've got a very long fuse. But this administration is really on
the verge of reaching the end of that fuse, and when I blow – man, there'll be
a lot of posts on this website! I mean it!

This week, President George W. Bush stated firmly that he would not
let the worldwide anti-war protests (which reportedly consisted of several
million people, several hundred thousand of those protesting from cities all
over the U.S.) affect his thinking about use of force in Iraq. He said, "It's like
deciding, well, I'm going to decide policy based upon a focus group."

I just have to say this: "No, it is not, you brainless, arrogant, inarticulate
gasbag." (The part after "No, it is not," I said under my breath, so as to avoid
getting sent to bed without dinner, or to prison in Cuba where my rights
to counsel and to confront my accusers, among others, would be illegally
withheld.)

Let me put aside my feelings about the war – whether I think it is
justified, whether I believe in Sadaam's supposed ties to Al Qaeda, whether
I feel Iraq poses a real danger to world safety – and focus on the facts of this
past weekend's protests. Millions of people all over the world have taken
their own initiative to peacefully show their opposition to the impending
war in Iraq. Even if this administration chooses to un-wisely ignore the
opinions of the rest of the world (and they have chosen this suicidal route
consistently since Bush's inauguration), there are still the hundreds of
thousands of protesters within our own borders to consider, nearly all of
which are concerned U.S. citizens. This is not a focus group, paid $100 for
their participation in a closed-room study of a new kind of yogurt aimed at
pre-teens and pregnant mothers. This is an upswell of public concern unseen

since the Vietnam war. This is people taking to the street, spilling off of the sidewalks, carrying signs and banners, bundled in thick layers to ward off the freezing cold (except in L.A., where we wore sandals), hoping to be heard, hoping to effect change. Even more telling, this protest is occurring before the war even happens! Nobody's died yet (at least not officially), and we are already protesting. Even the thick-skulled GWB, you'd think, must be able to see that this does not bode well for support of any war. Still, he seems smugly unconcerned.

My point is this – if we are really going to war to protect democracy and the freedoms that terrorists supposedly hate (for all of the current administration's policy is based upon the idea that terrorists hate freedom, not that terrorists are desperate individuals who can conceive of no better way to express their frustration over their poverty, oppression, ignorance and impossibly poor quality of life, and the perceived – and sometimes real – exploitation of these factors by uncaring, arrogant Western countries, of which the United States is the most visible symbol), if we are really going to war in defense of democracy, our administration should at least *acknowledge and respect the opinions of the people who elected them*. For that's what Bush's statement boils down to: he simply does not respect the opinion of the American people any more than he would the opinion of a paid focus group. Not only does our president not respect the opinions of the world and the world's leaders (at least not the ones who disagree with him), he does not respect the opinions his own people. Let me say it yet again: President George W. Bush does not respect the opinions of his own people.

Then again, maybe he's got a point. After all, we did elect *him* president.

Sort of.

Will It Never End?

Jeanette Scherrer   March 17, 2003

As a lesbian, and an atheist, and mostly as an intelligent woman, I am angry. First of all David: good point on how Bush won't base his decision for war on "focus groups" (i.e., anti-war demonstrations held by millions all over the world). A focus group is one gathered in a mall and paid $10 to try the new maxi pad with wings.

Warning: foul language ahead.

Two problems with the world are religion, and the fact that most of it is run by men.

First: I read a *Newsweek* article about the God-pushing George W. Bush. George purports that "the terrorists hate the fact that we can worship Almighty God the way we see fit." He thinks the "United States was called to bring God's gift of liberty to 'every human being in the world.'" He also believes that he was "called" to seek higher office. Are you fucking kidding me? He bases all his decisions on "someone" he can't hear, can't have a non-imaginary conversation with, can't see, or can't feel. We have a leader who absolutely believes he has a mandate from God to do what he's doing. What would we think if another country's leader now or in history said that? We'd think that person was crazy, dangerous, or both. Today that person is George Bush.

On another note, you all should know that last week in the House of Representatives in Washington state, two representatives, a man and a woman, walked out of a Muslim prayer led by the imam of the Islamic Center of Olympia. Their reasons? "Patriotism," one said, and the other cited "'lack of interest." How fucking stupid and ignorant!! First of all, there should be no prayer anyway. But, the Muslim priest was an American citizen, so I don't understand how he's unpatriotic. His prayer was a message of hope and peace. Lack of interest for hope and peace?

Also, *yay* to the upholding of not being able to say the Pledge in public school. If the mention of God (the Christian one) is not religious, then what is? This will go to the Supreme Court, who is always talking about the "spirit" of things when interpreting the Constitution. Well, the "spirit" under which God was added to the Pledge (no, it was not there originally) was during the Eisenhower reign, when it was decided that adding "under God" to the Pledge would be a good way to separate good U.S. citizens from the communist, godless Russians.

And a note on all the swept-under-the-carpet rapes at the Air Force Academy. Women who were raped who came forward were told that it was probably their fault, don't rock the boat, or to get over it. No, I'm not surprised. But this leads to the problem with men running the world. Women don't rape. Okay, there may have been that *one* time you think you heard of ... but please, any man who was raped by a woman – think about it – what a pussy. I bet the Air Force Academy would do something if men came forward because they were raped by a man or by a woman shoving a broomstick up their ass. Oh, yes, I'd bet there'd be some action taken then.

So let me ask you, how many wars have been started by atheists or women?

Days after the invasion of Iraq, I had to talk my sister out of a one-woman march from Mankato, Minnesota to Washington, D.C. She hoped she'd pick up other marchers along the way – it made sense to her at the time. You see, this war, the protests leading up to the war – these were Sara's first experiences as an activist. When the chips fell, and not where she expected them to fall, she wasn't sure what to do.

Frankly, I wasn't sure what to do either. I felt good about talking Sara down – any way you slice it, a solitary, pretty, relatively tiny girl walking the couple thousand miles from MN to DC was a bad idea. But I wasn't sure what to do about myself. I had never really been an activist either. Frankly, in my short adulthood, nothing this bad, on an international scale, had happened. This was, in a word, fucked.

What Now?

David Nett   March 25, 2003

I'm not sure what to write about this – how it will come out of me. I've even delayed the release of this week's edition of *CSP* because I think it is important that we say something. But, not just *anything*. Which is why I sit here, nervous and uncomfortable, as this stuff comes out of me in painful dribs and drabs.

We're at war now. And, just because the war has begun does not mean that I can stop being against it. That would be the easy road – the road that so many of our politicians have taken: they failed in their half-hearted attempts to prevent war, and now they "fully support the President and his decisions." I think I can do better than that. I think I can remain against the war, and firmly not behind President Bush, but still lend my support to those soldiers who are risking their lives in a fight that did not have to happen, at least not now. Some 20 or so U.S. and British soldiers are dead or missing. My heart goes out to them, to their families and friends. Those who are now in battle and those who will be soon – my support goes to you as well. May you be safe, may your job be done swiftly, and may you escape the war with as little physical and psychological damage as possible. The same goes to the Iraqi people – may you be safe, and come out of this intact. Now that we are in this war, the best way out is through swift resolution. I sincerely hope that our soldiers' jobs are completed soon – that we can oust the dictator, and begin the long, costly, painful and dangerous reconstruction effort as quickly as possible. Then, perhaps, we can turn our attention toward 2004 and the removal, through peaceful, legal elections, of our own despot.

But that begs another question. What *does* happen after the war? I think it's a foregone conclusion that the "coalition" (thanks for the support, Azerbaijan) will be victorious, though the time it'll take and the lives that'll be lost are yet unknown. But what then? This march toward war has done more than cause outrage in the Arab world, and in the hippie streets of California. It has splintered the United nations, the European Union and NATO. It has pitted ally against ally, and funneled great gobs of U.S. money through countries whose human rights abuses and terrorist-factories rival Saddam's own: Saudi Arabia, Turkey, Syria, etc. The march toward war has squandered, as former U.S. Diplomat John Brady Kiesling put it, nearly all of the international goodwill the U.S. has accumulated over the past few decades. After playing the bully for the past year, and making good on our threats in the past week, how will we convince our schoolyard chums that we're not going to tackle them when their backs are turned, that we won't hold them down and stuff dead leaves down their shirts, or make them eat mud? How will we fix the rift in the UN Security Council? In NATO? Or help Great Britain in the EU? Or repair the ill-will that has grown so strong in people throughout the world over the past year? I don't know these answers, by the way – I can't even begin to think how, apart from ousting our current leadership and starting fresh, we can even begin this healing. Our administration's arrogance, self importance, and blatant action only in their own interest, without respect for the interests and opinions of the rest of the world, has destroyed many international friendships in the past year and reduced our credibility as a nation of reason and, yes, justice, to all-time lows. Gawd help us if we don't find weapons of mass-destruction in Iraq, after all of this – if that happens, shit will really hit the international fan, and U.S. credibility will truly near zero.

Most of my real activist friends ("real," as opposed to "cyber," which is the comfortable, easy activism most of us engage in) have diverted their attentions now from direct opposition of the war effort to support of humanitarian aid and human rights groups. I think this is the right road to take. There are only a few people who can bring the war to a swift end now, and they are in Iraq, knee-deep in blowing sand, squinting through the dust at Baghdad. We must wish that they will be compassionate as they carry out their duties, and we should support, wherever we can, those who focus on helping the victims of war – those people who are wounded and displaced because of our actions, and their families and the families of those who are killed.

All this rambling. All this typing. All this liberal use of the delete key. And what, after all, am I saying? Just this: I do not support this war. Now that we are in it, I hope for swift resolution of it, with as little bloodshed as possible, and for the safety of our troops, who have been so carelessly placed in harm's way. I support doing whatever it takes, in both money and support, to heal Iraq once we've finished pummeling it to the ground. And I support the removal of those responsible for this blatantly unnecessary conflict – Bush, Cheney, Rumsfeld, and even Powell, as quickly as our democratic process allows.

With luck, the damage we've done to our reputation, to our friendships, to the UN, and to the idea of world peace, is not irreversible.

March Madness vs. War Madness

Jeanette Scherrer   March 25, 2003

I was all excited to wake up Thursday morning to plant myself in front of the TV for the beginning of March Madness, baby! Missouri (my alma mater) would be playing their first round game at around noon, and I was ready! Go Tigers! But what should happen? Somebody (this means you GWB) decided to start bombing Iraq, something I found very inconsiderate and inconvenient to all those NCAA tournament fans out there. Sure, they televised the games on ESPN, but not everybody has cable! GWB, certainly you have the current figures on the poor economy, and who currently can no longer afford cable. If you cut us, do we not bleed?

OK. So the war is news (barely). Sure Saddam Hussein experiments with chemical weapons on his own people. Sure he regularly murders Iraqis who speak or even think against him. Sure the Iraqi people don't see any of the fruits of all their oil. Sure his son, Uday, is a psychopath who regularly beats, rapes and murders women by the dozen, who has also killed members of his own family. But can any of them shoot a game-winning "trey" with .5 seconds left on the clock? I think not!

I mean, at least have two windows on the screen. One with the war and the other (larger) one showing hoops. It's the next day and they're *still* going on about that goddamn war. I mean, why didn't we finish this years ago with the other Bush? A double-elimination war is certainly not more exciting that the single-elimination NCAA tournament! One loss and you're out baby!

You'd think General Tommy Franks would be a hoops fan. I assume he's like, a man's man and whatnot, what with leading our entire armed forces into Iraq. I mean, what a better "who's dick is bigger" battle than the NCAA tournament? "Killing bad people," he may respond. But in the NCAA there's upsets abound. This war? A sure thing! You wouldn't watch a basketball game if you already knew who the winner was, right? So why is a war any different?

SPOILERS AHEAD:

Hey, the United States is going to win!

Now give me back my March Madness! Go Tigers!

(PS: No matter what my opinion is of this war, I do hope for the safety of our troops and the innocent people of Iraq.)

When Rick puts down the Xbox controller and writes a political essay, you know things are seriously off-kilter. It takes an especially heinous sort of activity to penetrate the thick Halo™ shield which constantly surrounds him.

Seriously, though, Rick's a great guy, and the liberal child, like me, of conservative parents, and he's a considerable danger with a joystick and a sniper rifle (not in a John Allen Muhammad way, of course). And, as you'll read in this essay, his eye was on John Kerry long before I had even considered him as a presidential contender.

Operation Eroding Freedom

Rick Robinson   April 8, 2003

In the new American landscape, where conservatives have seemingly cornered the market on patriotism and our liberal leaders have run to the hills, afraid of voicing criticism in the current political minefield, dangerous laws with innocuous names are being introduced, undermining the "enduring freedom" that are troops are trying to safeguard.

Oregon Senate Bill 742 has hit the floor and it seeks to re-define the term terrorist to include any person "who knowingly plans, participates in or carries out any act that is intended, by at least one of its participants, to disrupt: assembly, commerce and transportation." Breaking the proposed law listed above will result in being labeled a terrorist and sentenced to 25 years to life in prison. The language of the bill has since been changed by author Rep. John Minnis to include the phrase "violent acts," wisely excluding such noted terrorists as Mahatma Gandhi, who most certainly engaged in the disruption of transportation and commerce during his peaceful protests of Great Britain's occupation of India.

Admittedly, the bill is designed as a deterrent to demonstrators, a law created to give law enforcement "teeth" when dealing with unruly protestors who are undaunted by the misdemeanors with which they will likely be charged. Portland police have already starting fining vehicles for violation of a noise ordinance when they honked at peace protestors to voice their support.

Disturbingly, these protestors have started to be viewed as disrespectful to the troops who are fighting in Iraq, as if support of the troops and skepticism over our government's actions are mutually exclusive. This "muzzling" of the left by heavy-handed conservatives riding a crest of "rally around the flag" popularity is by far the most disturbing domestic by-product of the war in Iraq. Already we've seen dissonant artists and politicians lambasted for their critical comments of the commander-in-chief. Eddie Vedder was roundly booed at a concert in Denver for spiking a

George W. Bush mask on a his microphone, the Dixie Chicks boycotted by country radio stations for critical comments and Michael Moore demonized for the timing of his acceptance speech. John Kerry, speaking out at a time when most of his party is quiet, has said that America itself is also "in need a regime change," a remark that has come under heavy fire from his colleagues some journalists around the nation. It is important to note, that while the honorable Senators DeLay and Frist fire comments about being respectful to the men and women that serve our country, they themselves have never been in active military service, while Senator Kerry is a decorated veteran of the Vietnam War.

It is this backlash against free expression that is so troubling. Since when should we feel publicly condemned for taking to the street to oppose a war that we call into question? Since when is loving peace a slap in the face to our armed forces? There are hundreds of examples of court rulings where our basic freedoms were upheld over the safety of our citizenry. One needs only to look at the complex laws and long list of technicalities that a criminal can be acquitted on if proper police procedures are not followed. Is it beneficial to the public safety to let a likely criminal out onto the street because he was not properly advised of his Miranda Rights? No, but it is one of the many steps the government has in place to ensure that our freedoms are not infringed upon. What cost are we paying for all of this new security?

It is a time more than ever to cherish the freedoms that this country was founded to protect. Our humble beginnings can be traced back to the Boston Tea Party, an event that, if laws like Senate Bill 742 are passed, could be re-defined as a "violent act to disrupt commerce," and therefore, terrorism.

Triumph

David Nett   April 14, 2003

B aghdad has fallen, or, at least, nearly so. There will be continued fighting throughout the city and country for weeks and maybe months, certainly, but, since that team of American soldiers and Baghdad residents worked over Saddam's statue on his own Parade Grounds on Wednesday, Baghdad has effectively belonged to the Coalition.

Most of my friends and co-workers, Americans and Canadians all, are extremely happy the worst of the war appears to be over. Those who wanted the war wanted quick, decisive victory over Saddam, and got it, more or less. Those opposed to the war (like me) wanted it to stop as quickly as possible, with minimal loss of lives -- things went relatively well on that front, too (the lives that were lost, of course, were a needless waste in a war that never had to be, but that's another discussion...). But, as Coalition forces secure the rest of Baghdad and Iraq at large, hunt down and neutralize remaining resistance, and set up an interim government (which is bound to be rife with troubles – again, a discussion for another time), as the United Nations wrestles with the U.S. for a foothold in Iraq, and the U.S. Congress and Executive Office prepare another round of attacks on American civil liberties, we've forgotten about a very important question:

What about those Weapons of Mass Destruction?

They, after all, are the reason we went to war, right? I mean, as the push toward war went on, the Bush administration piled-on additional half-hearted reasons in a desperate attempt to win public and international support, liberation of the Iraqi people being chief among those, but the real reason, the root cause, were those weapons, right? Or, rather, Iraq's refusal to disclose the location, or even admit the existence, of those weapons. Our intelligence (granted, some good part of it was gathered from the public internet and various graduate student essays) showed the existence of "tons" of chemical and biological weapons, long-range missiles, and a budding nuclear weapon program.

So, where are they?

Look, I'm happy we haven't found them so far during the war, for "finding them" would probably have meant "being attacked with them," and that would be truly, truly terrible. But, now that we can sort of see the end coming, we'd better knuckle down and scrounge up some bad-ass weapons. When our administration went to the UN with our intent toward war, it was because we were certain these weapons existed, and that they threatened the security of the world, even though the inspectors had not found anything. They said that the Iraqi documents were incomplete, and that these secret weapons were such a threat that military action was required before they were used in an attack against us, or our allies. But, when the chips fell, Iraq didn't even use these supposed weapons in its own defense, which, while not exactly evidence that they do not exist, is at least enough to plant a seed of doubt. Hell, while I opposed the war, I never thought to doubt the existence of those weapons. Now I wonder.

Politically speaking, we could be in hot water if we don't find these weapons. Our credibility on the world stage is pretty low as it stands – if we don't find these weapons, France, Germany and others will again claim that this war was unfounded, that their proposed policies of continued pressure and inspection would have been as effective, without loss of life. And they'll be right. We won't soon recover from such a gaff, politically speaking. For the sake of America's political credibility, we must find those weapons.

And there's another problem. Not finding the weapons means one of three things: they never existed, they were destroyed sometime between 1440 and the war, or they were given to someone else, probably someone really, really nasty. There's bad political news for the U.S. if the first two are true, and bad, bad news for the entire world if the third is true. If our push toward war put "tons" of weapons of mass destruction in the hands of terrorists, who, as our occupation of Iraq continues, hate the U.S. and the rest of the West more and more, we are in deep shit.

I was/am against this war. I still think it was truly unnecessary, and I am skeptical about whether we can help to create a free, democratic Iraq anytime soon (though, if we do, that would be really wonderful). The purely ideological parts of me, which despise the unchecked ego and self-serving heavy-handedness of our current administration, would love to have my anti-war feelings vindicated by the revelation that our reasons for war were wholly unfounded. But the pragmatic part of me knows that we have to find those weapons, even if it means I was wrong. Too much rides on the proof of their existence, not only for the U.S., but for the continued security and stability of the world.

While many of us have spent some time in other countries (apart from frequent trips to Canada as a child, and infrequent vacations to tropical places, I spent some of my last year of college in acting workshops in eastern Europe), Jeremy is the only one of us who has lived overseas for any significant amount of time. He taught English in Asia, and worked as a Peace Corps volunteer for three years in Africa. He's currently helping to run a radio station in Kenya. In addition, he's traveled all over the world, and speaks a healthy fistful of languages.

From his vantage, he's better able to see the impact our actions have on the world at large and how the rest of the world views us.

Exporting God

Jeremy Groce   June 9, 2003

M ost Americans don't know much about international development.
The US is among the most developed (or you may prefer the term
"industrialized") nations in the world and most Americans view the rest
of the world as places not even worth visiting. This is unfortunate, in my
opinion, but this doesn't mean that I don't miss some aspects of American
life now that I am living in East Africa, specifically Nairobi, Kenya. For
instance, even here, after a long hard day of work I feel like relaxing and
watching a little television (make that "a little bit of television;" I actually
like my consoles big).

Back home in Iowa, I find that while many television programs are total
crap, there are some good ones. And then there are channels, like Discovery,
that I love, even if I don't enjoy every single one of their programs.

So I had heard that there is a channel in Kenya that airs programs
almost exclusively from the U.S. I was quite excited about this. After all,
while I love to watch local news and programs, I also like to be able to see
my favorite shows from home. When I learned what this channel really is
and saw it for the first time, I was sorely disappointed.

Let me back up a bit: Kenya has a lot in common with other countries in
Africa, like poverty and insecurity. However, Kenya has matured more than
many other African nations, especially in terms of democracy and a free
press.

Last December, Kenya elected a new president, Mwai Kibaki. Mr. Kibaki
defeated the candidate supported by the ex-president, Daniel arap Moi, who
finally stepped aside after nearly a quarter-century in office. The transition
to the new government has been peaceful and a cause for optimism, despite
a souring economy and mounting concerns over terrorism and security (the
terrorism concerns depress tourism, a vital part of the economy).

The defeat of the old ruling party can be contributed in large part to the fact that the population was better informed. They were also able to publicly demand change. These demands were transmitted via free, private media, including radio, print, and television. I am generally quite impressed with the quality of the media here, particularly print. The newspapers are robust and aggressive in their reporting.

Radio here is a mixed bag. While the news and music stations are generally of a high quality, too many stations sound like their signals are beamed directly from Chicago or Los Angeles. Many of the announcers put on these phony American accents and the promotions jingles and segues sound like they were produced by Rick Dees.

Television here is also a mixed bag. Some channels are quite good. Nation TV, part of Kenya's largest private media conglomerate, produces very professional programs, especially news programs. The others, particularly those owned by the state, are lacking. If you haven't seen television programs from a developing country, let me give you a general idea. Programs range from high-quality, like something you might see on C-SPAN, to medium-quality, like something produced by college TV stations, to low-quality, like the programs made by weirdos for airing on community access channels.

But the most disturbing television in Kenya comes from the good ol' U.S. of A. It's called "The Family Channel" and sometimes "Hope Kenya" and 24/7 airs some of the most shocking Christian-oriented programs I've ever seen. At times I am so fascinated, so terrified, by what's on this channel that I'll watch it for hours.

Most of the programs on The Family Channel are simply videotaped sermons, usually delivered by a fiery but pasty white preacher with a southern accent. Some of the preachers seem harmless enough, like the mustachioed Texas Baptist who preaches through hilarious stories. Others, like Benny Hinn, are downright dangerous in their "teachings."

The other night I was watching and came across a white-haired southern preacher whose name I don't know. He was talking about how evil homosexuality is and what an affront it is to God. He said that homosexuality is a choice, not a state, and that homosexual acts condemn those who commit them to hell. Nothing out of the ordinary, really, for the religious right.

Then he went on to defend mixed-race marriages, saying that all people are just people, regardless of skin color. "Rip these skins off our bodies," he said, "and we are all the same." I thought to myself, "Well, at least he's not a *total* bigot." Just as I finished this thought, the preacher went on.

"In a room you put a black baby, a yellow baby, a red baby, and a white baby. They all do baby things. They all make the same faces." He started making baby faces and then said, "If you give a toy to a black baby, he'll take the toy and do this." He then pantomimed dribbling a ball and shooting it, like a basketball into a basket.

"If you give the same toy to a red baby, he does this." He made a whooping sound and patted his mouth with his hand, creating the stereotypical Native American war cry from old movies.

Just then my power went out, turning the television off. By the time it came back on, the preacher was on to a new topic. I was very disappointed: I really want to know what the yellow baby and the white baby do with that toy. My wife, who's from Shanghai, joked with me that the yellow baby would use the toy to open up a Chinese restaurant. We really had no guess as to what the white baby would do.

Interspersed between these preachers' sermons are short, locally-produced segments that try to turn the messages just aired into cold, hard cash. There are usually three presenters, an older south Asian-looking and sounding man who seems to host these segments, a young portly American man with a shaved head who reads off lists of recently "saved" individuals (Kenyans), and an African woman (who sounds Kenyan) who does commentary.

With so many televangelistic broadcasts shown on The Family Channel, do the local donations get split amongst the preachers, or do they simply go into the coffers of whatever (presumably American) entity owns The Family Channel? I wonder because at the heart of these messages is some foul intent. The only question is whether the intent is simply to enrich the charlatan preachers, or if they have something more sinister in mind, because, in many respects, these preachers aren't much different than guys like Ayatollah Khomeini and Osama Bin Laden. We've started to see this already, with right-wing Christian terrorists killing abortion-performing doctors, blowing up gay night clubs, and the like. With the ever-expanding audience to which these dangerous men have access, the number of violent incidents is bound to multiply.

As a rule, I think religion can be a good thing. It can offer people a firm footing while navigating a life that is unpredictable and trying. Mainstream religions and their preachers offer people comfort and sound advice when they need it, as well as a forum for exercising the natural human need for spirituality. Unfortunately, there are plenty of people who take advantage of this need to create wealth and power for themselves. While the United States is busy fighting the war against terror, mostly in the Muslim world, I think we need to start looking very carefully at the terrorists' breeding ground in our own backyard.

I don't mean to be alarmist, but a world bombarded with messages of intolerance and religious absolutism can only become a more dangerous place.

And all I really wanted to do was to find re-runs of *Friends* on Kenyan TV.

GWB: Mandate from God

David Nett   June 23, 2003

It's hard to give enough time to local issues when the national and international situation appears so dire, and especially when, like with CSP, your readers (and other writers) are scattered throughout the country (and the world). But the national and international problems of tomorrow can sometimes be headed-off by dealing with them as local issues today, and today's local politicians are the pool from which tomorrow's governors and senators and presidents will be drawn. And, sometimes, a local issue can put a relatable face on a much larger social problem.

Los Angeles: Strike City

David Nett   October 20, 2003

Westlake Village, California – a predominantly wealthy suburb of Los Angeles (average house price in the mid $700k range), just inside the borders of L.A. County, where I work. Tacone – a trendy and expensive "healthy" sandwich shop at the Westlake Promenade. Lunchtime on a Friday. I'm in line to order a California turkey wrap, salivating in anticipation of fresh turkey and crisp vegetables wrapped in a homemade tortilla, all for only $8. Behind me, an older man of leisure, talking to his absurdly young, apparently recently be-boob-jobbed wife:

"Unions are the worst thing that ever happened to this country. They should just be happy they have jobs."

Sherman Oaks, California – like most of the San Fernando Valley (just outside of LA proper), a mix of the wealthy and the not-so-well-off, where I live. Trader Joe's – an independent food store chain, a little pricey, and the shop of choice for the well-off granola sect – not my usual supermarket. I'm in line to buy a few groceries. The lady in front of me – mid 60's, expensive and garish silk track suit, hideous visor and sunglasses, gi-normous jewel encrusted rings on her bony fingers – to the checkout lady:

"You're not on strike, huh?"

Checkout lady: "No."

"You're a good girl."

"Trader Joe's is non-union."

"Good for you. It's better to work here."

"Well, the insurance is okay if you work 40 hours or more, but we don't get paid nearly as much. It's not bad, but it's not very much."

"Well, you have a job at least – that's good."

"Yes."

I haven't been to my regular grocery store for about a week. United Food and Commercial Workers, who are employed at all of the major Southern California grocery store chains (Ralph's, Vons/Pavillions and Albertsons), are on strike (as they are in many cities across the country). The stores have hired non-union "scabs," but I, like so many other Angelinos, won't cross the picket line. The employees are not striking for better wages or more benefits. The final contract offered by those big store chains, rejected last weekend by the union, offered a dramatic reduction in starting wages and benefits for "new" workers (slowly increasing to the "established" workers' benefits over three years), and a slightly-less-than cost-of-living increase for current workers during that period, coupled with a 50 percent increase in employee-paid health care costs for families. For most workers with families, the insurance costs outweigh the meager increases, and the companies' hourly contribution toward these costs for those workers is so outpaced by the rising cost of healthcare that, after three years, they would bring home significantly less money than they do today. This could become an extreme reduction in compensation to an employee population which primarily hovers just above the poverty line, living paycheck to paycheck.

But the grocery chains are not the cause of the problem – their action is only a symptom of a larger illness. Yes, they are leaning heavily on their underpaid workers, which is wrong. But the grocery business margins are razor thin (two percent or less by some reports), and the industry is being squeezed.

The real problem lies in the insurance and healthcare industries. Especially in the past three years, a combination of escalating economic woes, rising energy costs, major catastrophes, and rampant, almost unchecked consolidation within the two industries has caused both the cost of basic health care and the cost of basic health insurance to skyrocket. As with so many other industries – telecommunications, the airline industry, energy production (Enron, anyone?) – the de-regulation watch-cry of "unregulated competition breeds lower prices and higher quality for consumers" has turned out to be dramatically false. Because of these drastic price increases, many companies find themselves forced to stop providing health insurance for their workers, and those who do continue to provide insurance often find the need to pass a greater cost onto their employees. States like California try to remedy the situation by mandating employee health coverage, but, since no one is watching the cost of such coverage, mandates like this, rather than really protecting the workers, just squeeze belabored businesses harder.

So, back to our striking grocery workers, who bear the brunt of these ill-conceived policies. With luck, they will prevail, and their new contract will, at least, reflect a continuation of the status-quo: continuation of current pay scales and insurance coverage at current costs. The grocery industry then, instead of squeezing it's employees, will hopefully turn to their representatives in congress, who are the only ones with the power to stop the ridiculous upward spiral of healthcare and insurance costs. Pressure will be applied upward, toward the federal government, looking for policy changes which provide real relief for business and workers, rather than downward, squeezing the life from hourly-workers, who are living largely hand-to-mouth.

Of course, the answer to all of this is not the one the Darwinian-capitalists in the current administration want to hear. Insurance costs are high not just because they are unregulated and corporations are greedy, but also because health care costs are so very high. Health care costs are high not just because the providers are unregulated and greedy, but also because new technology is expensive, government funding has been dramatically cut, and a flood of uninsured and under-insured cases forces higher costs on paying customers. It is becoming rapidly and abundantly clear that health care cannot be run coldly as a business like your neighborhood hardware store – healthcare is not hardware and a purely capitalistic mentality toward healthcare only disenfranchises those people who need it most. As demand increases, costs rise, but the ability to pay, in this crappy "jobless recovery" economy, decreases, and revenue drops, creating the need to raise costs ever higher, which increases the cost of insurance, which decreases employers' abilities to help pay for it, which decreases workers' coverage and ability to seek care, or pay for it when they do receive it. The cycle is vicious, and unending. A massive economic recovery and extended periods of economic boom, as in the mid-late 90s, mask the problem, since workers and employers, enjoying prosperity, can better afford to pay, but periods like the mid-late 90s do not last and, when those periods of wealth go away, the problem is again exposed.

The real (but painful to many) answer is universal healthcare – a healthcare system where society – the government and, ultimately, the taxpayer – provides basic, price-regulated health care for everyone who needs it. It's a jagged pill to swallow for many – it would require a massive effort on the part of all industries involved, and possible (but not certain) tax increases for some. And it is unlikely, in a time when our administration is more interested in making war than in providing basic necessities for its citizens. But, if we can find a way to gather for a universal healthcare plan even a fraction of the 150 billion dollars (or more) we're looking to spend in the first year or so of war, occupation and rebuilding in Iraq, and focus the national attention on the long-term benefits of such a plan, I believe a more enlightened administration can succeed. Howard Dean's proposals, as an example, would provide the opportunity for nearly every American to be protected by a regulated-cost plan very similar to that which members of congress enjoy. The estimated cost of such a plan: $88 billion – about the same amount which President Bush just requested to preserve the ongoing failure in Iraq.

I haven't all the answers, obviously. But I'm clear enough to recognize the real problem, and, if we can all stop pointing our fingers at overburdened worker, at the unions, and at corporations, many of which are struggling just as hard as you or me, that's a good start. The current healthcare fiasco is not the root of all our economic woes, obviously, but serious, effective healthcare reform could set in motion a series of dramatic, long-term economic benefits.

And, of course, it would give me the freedom to return to my local neighborhood grocery store once again.

We Are Liars and Traitors

David Nett   November 6, 2003

CBS has decided to pull the Reagan mini-series. We saw it coming – the attacks began in late October, as conservatives objected to the "historical inaccuracy" of the biopic, and *the Hollywood Reporter* saw CBS possibly cutting the four hour mini-series to a two hour, less objectionable, one night shot. The big network's dumping it altogether should not come as a surprise, especially in the face of threats of a campaign by the right against advertising during the show. While not surprising, CBS's action is still a tremendous blow to art and to free speech in general, and is just another example of a conservative suppression of dissent and open discourse by crying "liar" and "traitor."

A principle example of what was supposed to be objectionable about the Reagan mini-series was a statement made by Brolin-as-Reagan about the spread of AIDS: "They that live in sin shall die in sin." While conservatives cry "he never said that!" and the screenwriter herself replies that this is a fictionalized Reagan – apart from lines taken directly from public speeches, he may never have said *any* of these things, Reagan biographers agree that he may well have felt exactly that way. Regardless of whether Reagan really felt that homosexuals deserved AIDS (by the way, I know many hard-line conservatives who felt exactly that way and said as much, including my late grandfather, a Reagan Republican who served many years as a state legislator), the fact is that pressure from powerful conservatives was able to shut down a film critical of their greatest modern hero (my grandfather is also the man who convinced me, as a child, that Reagan's should be the fifth face on Mt. Rushmore) with an effort which lasted less than three weeks.

While Hollywood is in an uproar (ironic, since the mini-series, like most of its ilk, was likely to be cheesy and panned by most of those who are now defending it, albeit for its quality, not its content) over this blatant and frighteningly successful attempt to curtail creative freedom, I shudder at the larger implications. Ever since September 2001, conservative bullies and White House strongmen have been quietly or not-so-quietly quashing speech which does not sit with the presidential or conservative message. Whether it was branding those who preached caution about 9/11 retribution (like me) as "un-American," calling those who opposed the war in Iraq (again, like me), especially after it began, "traitors" to America and her soldiers, or blaming a "liberal media" for painting a grim picture of postwar Iraq, the current administration and its conservative following has made it a matter of policy to quash dissent and uncomfortable questions with a loud cry of "liar!" or "traitor!" rather than engage in civil debate. (When asked, at a press conference last week, if he could promise that by this time next year America would have fewer troops in Iraq than we now have, rather than talking about the future, President Bush said, "That's a trick question – I won't answer it.") When those simple tactics fail, they punish continuing dissent by exposing an undercover CIA operative, or by suing a former *SNL* writer. Rather than allowing *The Reagans* to air, and then examining it in an open forum, exposing whatever inaccuracies were to be found and correcting them with fact, conservatives screamed "liar" and bullied CBS into withholding it. Even the Showtime version, set to air next year, will likely be changed from what was meant to air next week, so we'll never really know what the hell they objected to, or whether those things made the final cut (this assumes that the bullies actually saw the show – most admit to be reacting to a short, seven-minute highlight reel – they don't appear to have any desire to actually watch the entire program before condemning it).

Surely nothing could be more American than the expression of contrary opinions and healthy debate over those opinions. And yet, with its policy of bullying and cries of "traitor," the current conservative movement, headed by the Bush administration, seems to want to squash that expression entirely. These conservatives don't think the American public can watch a television mini-series and not take every word of it as stone fact. They don't think the American people can hear two (or more) opposing opinions and choose for themselves the one that makes the most sense. They don't respect the average American enough to leave that choice in his or her hands. More ominously, they don't think the American people should hear opinions which contradict their views.

Fortunately, not all of us are answerable to big corporate interests and political pressure. And we say that Bush did not finish his work in the still dangerous, violent Afghanistan, that Bush's administration is illegally holding hundreds of prisoners in Cuba in violation of the Geneva

Convention, that he lied to us about WMD and Iraq's nonexistent ties to Osama Bin Laden in order to forward a war he'd planned since before his inauguration, that he and his broke the law in betraying an undercover operative, that his reckless economic policies (speaking of Reagan) have led dozens of states to financial ruin and put millions out of work, and that his imperialist aspirations have left us with an ongoing conflict in the middle-east which we can not afford to support, in terms of money or human lives. And that Reagan should not be the fifth face on Mt. Rushmore, no matter how big conservatives build his legend, or how much they decry those who draw attention to his flaws.

Unfortunately, *CSP*'s reach is somewhat smaller than CBS's. At least for now.

Michelle has the distinction of being the only self-proclaimed "conservative" among CSP's regular contributors. Still, despite her hard-line conservative positions on immigration and taxes, she could not find it in her to back George W. Bush the second time around.

Conservative Things

Michelle Magoffin   November 24, 2003

My mother was what some would call a bleeding heart liberal when I was growing up. And why wouldn't she have been? She was a young (very young) single mother of two trying to live and work in an expensive Southern California suburb because that's where most of our extended family lived. Were we poor? Probably not, but we certainly brought down the average annual household income for the area.

Over the years, and as our incomes have increased substantially, both my mother and I have found conservative ideas creeping into our political beliefs. I had no idea this was happening to her. I kept my status as a registered Republican a secret from my family for fear of starting a long, drawn out discussion in which my age would be the eventual determination of my ability to reason.

Then we started talking about the recall of Governor Gray Davis. We were both in favor of the recall but unsure of who to vote for to replace Davis.

The best thing that came out of the recall for me was a solidification of my views on certain topics and a re-ordering of my political priorities. I would likely say I am a moderate Republican, if forced to classify myself.

That is how Schwarzenegger described himself, but that is not why I voted for him. I voted for him out of pure strategy. I did not want Bustamante to win. I liked Tom McClintock for governor, although he is much more conservative than I will ever be. I thought he had the experience and the vision to overhaul what I saw as the problem areas (fiscal) in the state. The issues on which I disagreed with him (social) were not likely to arise during the remaining three years of this gubernatorial tenure and were not of utmost importance to me.

That is what makes me leery of calling myself a Republican. When it comes to some social issues, I have liberal views. Pro-choice: of course.

Gay marriage: fine by me. Equal rights for any American who wants them: doesn't hurt me any. Environment: we should probably preserve that. Death penalty: well, this is where it starts to get tricky. I am in favor of the death penalty and I think that more crimes should have a capital penalty. Child molesters, rapists, torturers; why should these people not pay the same price as murderers? To me, their crimes are much more reprehensible.

Illegal immigrants: most of my views on this huge topic stem from how I feel about being a law-abiding citizen. For the longest time, I wanted to work for either the CIA or the FBI. To that end, I made sure that I never broke any law or engaged in any behavior that would jeopardize my chances. I feel strongly that people should abide by the law and if a law needs changing, work within the system to change it. To that point, I think that anyone who breaks the law should be punished accordingly. Illegal immigrants are breaking the law by being in this country and they are bypassing the legal methods that thousands of immigrants are using to legally reside in the U.S. Because of this fundamental belief, I do not support any legislation that affords rights and services to illegal immigrants. I do, however, feel strongly that our immigration policies need to be revisited and reformed to allow more people to enter the U.S. legally, to make the process less onerous, and to close security loopholes.

These views put me well on my way to being a card-carrying fan of Rush Limbaugh (I shudder to think). The only major issues left to consider reside in the fiscal arena and this is where my Republican really starts to show. I will admit that some of this is selfish. I want to keep as much of my paycheck as I can, even if it is at the cost of social programs for the homeless, the jobless and the uninsured.

It is unfathomable to me that state government should be so opaque. It makes more sense that government should be run using a corporate model. If a corporation ran a deficit the size of the one the state of California has, it would be on its way out of business and people would be fired. The board of directors would bring in a clean-up team and perform audits. The audits would reveal redundancies in offices and programs, hemorrhaging of assets, and just plain criminal behavior. This seems like common sense to me but, it turns out, this is called "fiscal conservatism" and was denounced, decried, and denied during the recall campaign, primarily by the Democrats.

I have no stunning conclusion here. I am conflicted by my own beliefs.

They are, in fact, relatively new to me. Up until a year ago (right after Davis was elected governor), I was apathetic and uninformed about most things political. I clung to the lofty ideals of my adolescence and did not give much thought to how they translated into reality. I am becoming more involved in these messy, political issues and will likely have shifting views as I sort out previously unexamined minutiae. In the meantime, I like to talk to people who disagree with me to find out how they came by their beliefs, but I do not like to debate the merits of one view over another. I am not at all interested in converting others to my way of thinking or in proving that my point is right and someone else's is wrong.

At least not about politics.

I love Jeremy like a brother. In fact, as I was the oldest of four kids, he was kind of a big brother to me throughout much of my adolesence. And, as is always the case with brothers, we've had our disagreements – sometimes even violent ones.

I remember one time we were playing Dungeons and Dragons, and Jason, Martinsen and I (John or Goldy may have been there, too – I don't recall) were teasing Jeremy pretty hard. He suddenly exploded out of his chair, upsetting the table, throwing books and dice everywhere, and spilling my massive Big Gulp on my lap. "I'm taking my books and leaving!" he shouted, and he did, except leaving just meant going into his room and slamming the door, since we were at his house.

To be fair, they were his books, and we were being total dicks. But that's no reason to pour Coke all over my favorite pair of Hammer pants.

The Reagans: David Overreacts

Jeremy Groce   December 29, 2003

I usually agree with my good friends who are fellow contributors to the *CSP* website. However, recently I read an essay, written by Dave, that I thought deserved a rebuttal. We'll see if Dave publishes this or not. I know he will, but it would certainly be ironic if he didn't (you'll understand why if you read his essay). The essay in question, by the way, is *We are Liars and Traitors*, written about CBS network's decision not to air a mini-series about the Reagans.

The decision by CBS, a privately-owned company, to pull the plug on the Reagan mini-series is hardly "a blow to art and free speech," as Dave characterized it. CBS simply responded to market forces and elected to avoid controversy. The decision may have been cowardly, but it's hardly censorship. If the Bush administration had pressured the FCC to threaten CBS with revocation of license or some such thing if it aired the mini-series, then we could label it an act of censorship.

When MTV chose not to air a Madonna video in 1990, she told Nightline's Ted Koppel that she was being "censored." Again, MTV is a private company and they can choose to air or not air what they choose. Interestingly, Nightline aired the video to show their viewers what all the fuss was about. Too racy for MTV, but not for ABC, apparently.

Clearly, any show about Ronald Reagan is going to be controversial. His administration is not ancient history. Many Americans have very strong feelings – one way or another – about the Reagan years. CBS was probably being naive to think a movie about a politically conservative icon with James Brolin and Judy Davis in the lead roles would not rustle some feathers.

To be fair, CBS should have tried to ensure that a movie about Reagan would be balanced. He and his family members are still living (though he is so ill he is unable to defend himself). Those who worked with and for him are still alive and well, many still in government. Can't CBS make sure that they don't air a hatchet job? In fact, the series contains some episodes of dubious historical accuracy. While it is true that Reagan may have said something like "they that live in sin shall die in sin" with regards to AIDS victims, his biographers say that he certainly did not supply names to the Hollywood blacklist of communists, as the mini-series claims. And according to one article I read, in the miniseries Reagan refers to himself as "the Antichrist," in case we miss the point.

The writers and producers say they are merely taking the literary licenses required to make a good television drama. But many will ask why literary license must be taken at all when dealing with such recent events, much less dealing with a beloved former American president who is still living. For example, there is virtually no historical evidence to illuminate the real nature of the Thomas Jefferson/Sally Hemmings relationship. As such, writers have taken more liberties and concocted all kinds of stories about them, including some that I have found offensive. But Mr. Reagan, his wife, his children, friends, etc. are still alive. What did the folks at CBS think was going to happen?

Now, I'm not saying that the miniseries should not air. I'm only saying that under these circumstances, CBS should have understood that many advertisers would be wary of this program. Further, they are perfectly within their rights to object to this program and say they will not advertise with CBS if the network goes forward with the broadcast. And CBS is within their rights to take that information into account as it decides what to air and what not to air.

For those who think I'm letting CBS off the hook, let me suggest an alternative scenario. Let's say that a network decides to air a program about Anne Frank. Only in this version, she holds some Nazi sympathies and tries to sneak out of hiding in order to bed a young Aryan soldier in order to produce "half-pure" children. She says she can't tell any of her family of this feeling because she knows they wouldn't understand. She starts to write about it in her diary, but crosses it out because she's too embarrassed.

A writer could say he is simply taking some literary licenses in order to make the story "more dramatic." After all, the old Anne Frank story has been told a million times. "Time to add some ol' sex and pepper to the tale," he tells TV Digest.

Think of how outraged and offended the world would be by this program. Think of the protests that would be organized. Advertisers and many other groups would rally and would demand that the network not run the mini-series. In all likelihood, the network would relent and the show would be shelved (or burned).

As a former president, Ronald Reagan is a prime candidate for a biopic, no doubt. But because there are so many people who love him and many who most definitely do not love him, let's leave it to the History Channel to do a show about his life, not CBS.

When I think about the supposed "conservative drift" (or, as I have recently heard it called, the "new morality," which makes me throwup a little bit in my mouth) in the U.S., I immediately think of my close friend (and CSP contributor) Jeanette. I'm a middle-class heterosexual white male and, while I'm outraged at blatantly discriminatory proposals like an anti-gay-marriage constitutional amendment, such a thing would not directly affect me (except in the sense that the sanctioning of such bald-faced bigotry diminishes us all). Jeanette, on the other hand, would be suddenly constitutionally prohibited from marrying someone she loved. It makes me incredibly sad to think that current conventional widom holds that, in America, she is considered, by most people, a second-class citizen.

Fortunately, I don't think conventional wisdom is entirely correct in this case. While a majority of Americans do currently (whether out of fear or misguided religious fervor) oppose homosexual marriage, according to many polls, only a minority would vote for such a constitutional amendment. The only explanation for this that I can see is that that a large portion of those who oppose gay marriage realize that their position is irrationally discriminatory, or that, given the right circumstances, their opinions could be swayed. Those people do not want to permanently enshrine their bigotry in our great nation's most important document.

I'm Gay, I'm Frustrated, and I Don't Want to Get Used to It

Jeanette Scherrer   January 23, 2004

So being the only gay person contributing to *CSP* (or the only "out" one, I should say, oh yes, you all know who you are), I feel like writing about gay stuff. The following will probably have no point and ramble here and there and on and on, so it's okay to read it piecemeal, when you're on the toilet, etc.

Recently David sent me an article by a right-wing whacko Christian defending those brave "soldiers" who kill doctors who perform abortions. This guy was going on and on and suddenly, out of nowhere, in talking about the heinous sin of killing unborn babies, he had to throw in how equally horrible homosexuality was!

I'm frustrated, to say the least. I know people are blind and ignorant, and that most of their decisions or beliefs come out of fear, mostly fear of the unknown. People believe in a "god" for fear that they'd have to look at their short life, where out of fear they probably didn't take the risks they should have to pursue their dreams. They hope to hell there's an afterlife. They desperately need this afterlife or reward of "heaven" so they don't have to look at themselves and see how they've pissed their life away, and contributed nothing to the world.

I understand fear of the unknown, of things you're not used to or don't understand. I'm from a small town in Missouri – about 3,000 when I lived there. And I remember judging people by their cover, people of different color and ethnicity, people with piercings or tattoos, people who dressed differently, because it wasn't what I was used to. So my first conclusion must be that people hate or are afraid of homosexuals because they don't know any and have certain ideas and stereotypes in mind.

I was reading a *New York Times* article that I knew would piss me off, and it did. It was an article talking about the recent Massachusetts Supreme Court ruling that said there is no legal reason to keep homosexuals from getting married. It is illegal to give a certain group of citizens rights and privileges and not give those rights to another. Whether I want to ever get married or not, it's the principle of the matter. I won't stand for anything less than full marriage rights. Not this appeasing domestic partner bullshit, which is "everything but", because that still implies that I am still lesser than, less deserving of, not equal to heterosexual people.

I know what people are afraid of. Let's get down to it. People in this society are sexually repressed. Men, I think, have more of a problem with homosexuality than women do. Straight men are terrified that if they're not looking, and if a fag is near them, they're going to end up with a dick in their ass. You may laugh, but it's true. It's the whole dick in the ass thing that freaks them out. Two dicks, two assholes, it's like some new math. But how many of them have begged a woman to let them fuck her in the ass? *Lots.* How many straight men like a finger, butt plug or dildo in their ass for that prostate stimulation? How many men would like to experiment? Lots. But if a straight guy went to a party and told his straight guy buddies, "Yeah, I sucked dick and took it in the ass for a while, but it was just a phase," well, good luck with them being open to that. Some don't want anything in their ass, like my good, straight friend Dwayne, his ass is "exit only", but there are *many* others who do want that.

Why do women hate homosexuals? What is your problem? You have nothing to fear from gay men. They won't treat you as objects, they won't paw you in a bar, and they don't want to get their dick in you just to use you or get off. So you can't have a problem with them. Maybe it's the lesbians they're afraid of. Have they been chased by a lesbian with a strap-on? The worst thing that could happen is that they meet a lesbian who wants to go down on them for hours and then hold them afterwards and talk about their feelings. Need I say more? And don't get me started about men and two women. You all think that's hot, whether you admit it or not. You just get pissed when those two women can a) beat you at arm-wrestling and b) don't want your dick in the equation.

So what's the fear? In that *Times* article a woman said that if she had gay neighbors she wouldn't let her kids go over there because homosexuality can be "acquired." I just want to punch that woman. I don't want to get to know her, I don't want to reason with her, I just want to hit her. That's my frustration with the sheer ignorance. My parents are straight, but I didn't acquire that. The books I read were always from, about, and as far as I knew, written by heterosexuals and imposed a view of a straight-only society. That didn't change me.

Then there's the whole god thing. And the "I don't hate the sinner, just the sin." I don't even know how to respond to that. Be gay, just don't act on it? That's the direct result of a sexually repressed society thinking it's okay and healthy to suppress the most powerful driving force in nature. I can't even get into how many problems are manifested in this society by the suppression of natural, *healthy* (I don't mean the rapists or child molesters) sexual desires. All I have to say is "judge not lest ye be judged," "love thy neighbor as thyself." Hey all you homo-haters out there. If a man loves a man ... hell, if a man fucks a man or a woman licks another woman's pussy, and if it's between two consenting adults, how does it effect your life? Oh, sorry, it makes you uncomfortable? Well isn't that your problem?

I don't know what I'm trying to say. I ask gays, lesbians, bisexual, transgendered (and that's one people *really* can't deal with), for god's sake, be proud of who you are. You know, be *out*. Be happy with yourself.

But mostly I *beg* the straight people. We homosexuals, being a minority, can't change people's perception and thinking on our own. We need more than tacit support. If you hear someone talking prejudice or hate language about gays, speak up. That goes triple for homosexuals themselves. For those of you who know me, or know someone else who is your friend who is gay, stand up for them.

My friend Dwayne is black, and I tell you whether he's around or not, if I hear someone say the word "nigger" in a 100-mile radius, I'm ready for a fight, because it's *wrong*.

GWB: Mission to Mars

David Nett

February 12, 2004

Before we start today, I wanna say that I know that many of you have questioned my recent decision to begin a program aimed at first colonizing the moon, and then putting a man on Mars. This may seem espe...especi..really a puzzler considering all the problems we have here at home, with the deficits and job loss and whatnot. Well, let me say this:

Our intelligence agencies have learned that the Martians have attempted to purchase weapons-grade Dilithium from Uranus. In addition, we have definitive proof that Mars has stockpiles of Weapons of Universal Distruction, including Phasers, Disruptors, Tachyon Cannons, and Cloaking Devices, and could launch an attack on Earth with as little as 45 nanoseconds preparation.

In addition, it has come to our attention that the Martians have been feeding steroids to our athletes, threatening to reverse my tax-cuts, and infecting decent, God-fearing Americans with the Gay, and forcing them to sue for marriage rights. In light of all of this, it would be irresponsible for us not to take steps to invade ... er ... land a man on Mars! The War on Terror demands that we take this next logical step!

Remember, you have to agree with me -- I'm a war-time president.

Craig came to CSP with two pieces ready to be published. This was one of them. At a time when I'd all but lost my sense of humor about politics, Craig reminded me that laughter is often the best teacher. For a good while, this was the most visited essay on CSP, and it still remains among the top few. Reading it, you will quickly see why.

Breaking Up With America

Craig Bridger   February 19, 2004

Look. It's not you. It's me. No really. It's my problem. America, listen. Listen to me. God, you're beautiful. This is so hard for me.

I think we should spend some time apart. No, there's no one else. No, I am not in love with Canada. How could you think that? Yes, she has a very nice health care system, but that's not the point. I'm not comparing your murder rate with Britain. Don't be silly. You have a very sexy murder rate. Nobody can compare with your murder rate, you know that. What? Of course I don't think France is smarter than you. Why does it always have to be about France? Well, I'm not calling them "freedom" fries because that's just silly. Please, you have to stop with this French thing.

You see, that's just what I'm talking about. I can't disagree with you about anything. I can't have my own opinions. It didn't used to be that way with us. We used to talk to each other, but you won't listen to me anymore. And you've found God – which, I think is great, really – but you're so self-righteous all the time. You're so judgmental. Well, I'm sorry, but it's true. Anybody who you don't like is "evil." It's embarrassing. You can't talk to people like that. And stop blessing yourself all the time, for crying out loud. You bless yourself more than the Pope!

What's that? Traitor? Oh, that's good, who taught you that, Ashcroft? You know, who the hell are all these new friends of yours, anyway? Well, I'm sorry, I've tried to get along with them, but they're just assholes, America. And you know something? All of our old friends think so too. That's right. Nobody can stand to be around those jerks. And you've turned into one of them. That's why we didn't get invited to Nick and Lori's party this year. Well, let's see, last year, you cheated at Monopoly, hogged the guacamole, got wasted, and took a dump in Lori's tub, remember?

Oh, you're one to talk, Missy. That really takes the cake. I'm a liar? Hi "Pot," this is "Kettle" calling. Everything that comes out of your mouth is a lie. You've told me so many lies I've forgotten what the truth sounds like:

"The moon is made of green cheese, the world is flat, war is peace, snakes don't have ears, mercury is good for you, I can do six hundred sit-ups," I mean, who knows? Who knows what to believe anymore? I don't! That's fine! Throw me out! Good, have Rumsfield over, fine! I'm moving in with Canada! She understands me! *We're in love!*

Look, I didn't want to do this. I didn't want to fight with you. I'm sorry, America. I don't know, I don't think we should talk for a while. If you want, you can e-mail me. It's monitored? Well, *whose fault is that?*

Hello?

Christ.

Matrimonial Discrimination

David Nett   February 24, 2004

O kay – I seriously cannot take this anymore. I want everyone to take a step back, just for a second, and realize that a Constitutional amendment banning gay marriage is the most serious, widest-reaching form of governmentally sponsored discrimination I've seen in my lifetime (I'm 30). I mean it – drop your fake moral posturing. Take off your conservative religion-colored glasses. There is no real, fundamental need for anything of this sort. A Constitutional amendment encouraging discrimination, based upon the shifting sands of religious-based moral fervor, of fear-based prejudice, of traditionalist ignorance – surely this is a nightmare, and I will wake soon. George W. Bush, court-appointed President of the United States: you, sir, have gone too far.

You see, this goes way beyond typical presidential politics. Laws, executive orders, between-session judicial appointments – these can all be overturned, and relatively easily if public opinion is behind the move. Even those laws and orders with ongoing popular support can be circumvented administrationally through withholding funding, etc. (just look at what Bush has done to Clinton's popular environmental work). But Constitutional amendments are a much different animal. Overturning a Constitutional amendment is not technically possible – all that can be done is the ratification of another amendment which includes language repealing the prior amendment. This has only been done, to my knowledge, once – the 21st amendment repealed the 18th (Prohibition). Amendments, for all practical purposes, are permanent. Even an "overturned" one remains forever a part of the Constitution.

Writing discrimination into the Constitution would place a terrible blemish on the face of the most important document under United States law. All of the other current Constitutional amendments are clarifications of points of law, rules establishing the inner workings of the executive and legislative branches, and declarations of freedom from discrimination and oppression (Article XIII makes slavery illegal, Articles XV, XIX, XXIV &

XXVI make certain that everyone over 18 can vote). This newly proposed Constitutional amendment would be the first to sanction discrimination.

And, interestingly, this propsed amendment is in direct opposition of Article I, commonly called the "First Amendment." We normally think of the First Amendment as the Freedom of Speech amendment, but what we often forget about is this little gem:

"Congress shall make no law respecting an establishment of religion."

This is one of the basis for the expression "separation of church and state." Basically, it prohibits the creation of laws based upon the edicts of one religion or another. There are two arguments I've heard for the banning of gay marriage – the first, and often loudest, is that homosexuality, and the expression thereof, is against God's will. If we pass a law based upon this assumption (which is held only by some faiths, not by all, not by a long shot), we are directly violating the first amendment (in this sense, Clinton's Defense of Marriage Act is unconstitutional – Bush knows this, and has hinted at its vulnerability to being overturned). In passing a Constitutional amendment banning Gay marriage on these grounds, we are effectively repealing a portion of the 1st Amendment.

The second argument against gay marriage is far weaker than the first, but has more purchase in the current debate, because most opponents of Gay marriage, who in their hearts oppose it for reason number 1 (above), *know* that their reasoning is unconstitutional, so they've created this second argument to mask their faith-based discrimination. The second argument: gay marriage flies in the face of tradition, and damages the foundation of the American family.

The response to this argument is simple: tradition is not always right. The tradition of slavery, held for thousands of years, was wrong, and eventually we came to see that. The tradition of treating women as second-class citizens, held pretty much since the dawn of human civilization, was wrong, and eventually we (most of us) came to see that. The tradition of prohibiting mixed-race marriages was wrong, and eventually we (again, most of us) came to see that. All of these "traditions" helped define how the American family worked, in their time, and the breaking of these traditions was right and necessary, despite the inevitable changes to the "traditional American family," because discrimination, in all forms, is wrong, and is a cancer that eats at the heart of society.

The reality is that there is no argument to defend a ban on gay marriage, anymore than there is an argument for any other form of arbitrary discrimination. The only reason we are even debating this is because homosexuals are the last well-defined group in America against whom it is still "okay" to discriminate. As with all other forms of discrimination, this has its roots in ignorance and fear. As we grow as a society we will come to realize that, whatever the Pope says, whatever our bibles tell us (remember, our Bibles tell us that a wife must obey her husband, and that slavery is a-okay), homosexuality is not a crime, any more than it is a simple lifestyle choice. Homosexuals are who they are, and they deserve the same rights and freedoms as every other human being. This proposed Constitutional amendment is nothing more than dangerous, divisive political posturing in an election year, by a President whose (nearly) every action in office has been dangerous, divisive, or both. The biggest problem with this gesture is not the petty, narrow-minded, short-term goals of this little man who runs our country, but the permanency of a Constitutional Amendment. This is why we should fight Bush's proposal with all our strength. I think the American people will see this, will understand this. I hope they will.

The American family will endure gay marriage. The people will come to realize that the foundation of the American family is not one man and one woman who procreate and raise their biological children together – it is mutual love and respect between people who support each other emotionally, socially and sometimes financially, who sometimes decide to pledge their lives to each other, who sometimes decide to raise children (their own or others who need love), who contribute to society by providing a network of human connection which spreads across our country and the world. The American family is evolving, and always has been. Gay, straight, black, white, brown, male, female and everywhere in between – the only truly important constants are love and respect.

No Leg to Stand On

Jeanette Scherrer   March 8, 2004

I have to tell you, when I got up on Tuesday, February 24, 2004 and read the CNN headline about Bush wanting a Constitutional amendment banning gay marriage, I cried. I cried because I was angry and because I was frustrated.

First, there's the religious, so-called moral argument. But you can't make laws based upon religion. The First Amendment states, "Congress shall make no law respecting an establishment of religion"

Let's go there anyway, because there's no arguing with people on a religious basis because if it's wrong in the bible then it's wrong. Let me use their own arguments against them. They say homosexuality is wrong because (they think) it says so in the bible. Biblically speaking, adultery is also wrong. Still, it is everywhere. It's even a commandment! Eight or more times in the bible it talks about adultery: a married person can't have sex with a person who isn't their spouse. You're also not supposed to have sex outside of marriage.

It also talks specifically about divorce. Divorce isn't allowed, but if you do get divorced you can't get remarried because the first marriage is sanctioned by God and it's a union "that no man can put asunder." That bond is broken only in death of the spouse. So if it says it's wrong in the bible it must be wrong. How many of you who are against gay marriage are divorced or were virgins when you got married? I mean these are major no-nos in the bible. You guys are going against the teachings of God and Jesus, big time. Why aren't you trying to pass an amendment disallowing divorce? Isn't it divorce that's causing the breakdown of marriage? Of course it is, because divorce destroys a marriage. Will allowing a gay couple to marry directly cause you, the hetero married couple, to divorce?

And slavery is accepted in the bible. In the Epistle of Paul to the Ephesians: "Slaves, obey your human masters with the reverence, the awe, and the sincerity you owe to Christ." In the Epistle of Paul to Timothy:

"All under the yoke of slavery must regard their masters as worthy of full respect, otherwise the name of God and the church's teaching suffer abuse." And my favorite, in the First Epistle of Peter: "You household slaves, obey your masters with all deference, not only the good and reasonable ones but even those who are harsh."

Wow! Pro slavery and anti-adultery are all over the bible. Why aren't you all trying to pass laws promoting slavery and condemning adultery and divorce? From what I understand if it's in the bible then that's it, that's what you believe. "Oh, well we don't have to listen to that part, everybody knows slavery is wrong." Hmm. So you get to pick and choose? By the way, "Why do you look at the speck in your brother's eye when you have a plank in your own?"

I am a taxpaying American citizen. You were born right-handed, I was born left-handed. You were born heterosexual, I was born homosexual. Some of you say it's a choice, that Jeanette can get married to a man any time she wants. Fine. So then straight males can easily choose to be sexually attracted to a man. No? Oh, then I guess it's not a choice. Why should I be denied (even with a civil union) more than 1,000 federal tax benefits that the hetero drunk couple who just met and got married in Vegas are instantly entitled to – no questions asked?

And let me briefly talk about homosexuality being unnatural. How can it be unnatural when there have always been homosexual people? And by the way, do an internet search and you'll find that there are many documented cases of homosexual behavior even in the animal kingdom. Some say gays shouldn't get married because they can't naturally have children. So therefore the hetero men and women who are sterile shouldn't get married, right?

There are no good arguments against gay marriage. The big problem, for people against it, is that they find the thought of a man with a man or a woman with a woman uncomfortable or disgusting or unnatural, a fear of what they don't understand. Most people against it don't know anyone who's gay, and certainly have no close gay friends. How will a gay couple who want to commit their lives together adversely effect your straight marriage?

People say that children of gay parents have a harder time. The only reason they do is because the children who do the teasing are taught by their parents that it isn't wrong. Children aren't born with hate and intolerance of others. Some say gay parents shouldn't have children because the kids will turn out gay. That's just stupid. All the gay and lesbian people I know have straight parents. All my education, all the books I had to read in school, was all taught from a straight perspective, and it didn't "turn" me straight.

Denying homosexuals right to marry is legally wrong. If you don't want gays to marry, then allow civil unions for everyone, and leave the term marriage where it belongs, in the religious institutions. But the fact is marriage is a legal institution. State and federal governments recognize it as such and give tons of tax breaks to married couples. So it is a legal contract, and The Constitution of the United States, Amendment 14, says, "No State shall make or enforce any law which shall abridge the privileges or immunities of citizens of the United States; nor shall any State deprive any person of life, liberty, or property, without due process of law; nor deny to any person within its jurisdiction the equal protection of the laws."

You may say, "Well, don't worry, Jeanette, such a constitutional amendment will never pass." Maybe, maybe not. Bush said this to appease his conservative, religious constituency. He said it to take focus away from all his other shortcomings and failures. The fact is, gay marriage evokes a strong emotional and visceral response in people. For the most part, all the other issues: jobs, health care, the non-existence of WMD's, do not evoke such a response. Don't think for a minute the people won't cast their vote for or against the idea that effects them strongest emotionally, and in this election it is gay marriage.

I've heard people say the homosexuals should keep their mouths shut about this issue before they ruin the election for the Democrats. I say, why should I go one more day, one more minute as a lesser citizen? They said the same thing to women about their right to vote. "Oh, now's really not a good time."

The fact is there have always been, and always will be, homosexuals.

Face it, you can't discriminate or hate us out of existence.

As the race to pick a democratic presidential nominee began, I quickly became a member of the Howard Dean camp. I'd never been a huge Kucinich fan, despite our similar ideals, and apart from him Dean was the only real anti-war candidate. As the campaign dragged on, I also became enamored of both Edwards and Kerry, for different reasons. I soon came to realize that all of the front-runners were a bit more conservative than I'd have liked, but I believed any of these three would make a fine president.

When Dean stumbled in Iowa (or, rather, when the media decided that Dean had stumbled), and Kerry's policies (as reflected on his website) began to really solidify, I knew he'd be my new candidate of choice. His Vietnam-era politics appealed to me, and I appreciated his courage, his record of uncovering corruption in the Senate, his healthcare proposals, and his thoughtful (if a bit hawkish for my taste) approaches to Iraq and the "War on Terror." He also seemed, next to George W. Bush (with his abominable first-term record in almost every area, from the economy to the environment to foreign policy), an almost idyllic candidate. Almost.

The Real L-Word

David Nett   March 11, 2004

Predictably, the smear campaign has already begun. The current administration's guns have been turned on John Kerry, the Democratic party's likely Presidential nominee, for the past couple of weeks. But those guns are filled with less ammo than in the past – in the past, those guns have been loaded with some heavy-duty ordinance: "Soft on Crime," "Draft Dodger" (hello, pot – this is kettle), and so on. This year, the ammo box is looking a little low. This year, the Right's entire salvo seems likely to consist of one shot fired over and over again: John Kerry is a ... Liberal.

Gasp.

At some point in our history, the label "Liberal" became political death. The Right flings it at the Left like poisoned javelins. The Left try to dodge, to bob and weave their way away from the hated word. Even proud Liberals run, because those that don't are skewered (Dukakis, anyone?) by public perception. The "Liberal" label, in our current political climate, is one to be avoided at all costs. At some point, in the collective public understanding "Liberal" came to mean "elitist." The fact is, nothing could be further from the truth:

Liberal means Acceptance.

A lot of people will tell ya that Liberal means "tolerance." In a society whose perception is so shifted to the Right that it's okay to pass legislation based upon religious doctrine and hold suspected criminals indefinitely without benefit of charge, legal counsel or trial, sometimes tolerance seems to be the best we can hope for for our marginalized communities – our women, our elderly, our racial minorities, our religious minorities, our homosexuals, our working poor. But real Liberalism is more than just tolerance of those who are different. Real Liberalism accepts and embraces our differences. Real Liberalism includes all of our communities into a larger American community. Tolerance means that we can live in proximity with each other and continue on our paths without overt hatred or violence, which is great. But "acceptance" means we include each other, that we weave our lives together, and that all parties grow stronger for the support of each other.

Liberal means Equality.

This follows logically after the acceptance above. It's great to accept people's differences – it's quite a lot harder to treat everyone, regardless of differences, equally. It's especially hard to fight for equality for those who are different from you. This is what real Liberals do. They know in their hearts that everyone deserves equal treatment under a just legal system, and they fight to make those equalities a reality. Sometimes that involves doing something initially unbalanced (like giving extra advantages to a traditionally oppressed group) to try to speed the process of leveling the playing field. But a true Liberal realizes that that short-term sacrifice provides real long-term benefits. In a society of equals, the fundamental causes of violence and poverty begin to melt away.

Liberal means Social Responsibility.

Liberals understand that we have a basic human responsibility to our fellow man, to our environment and our international community, as well as to ourselves. We are part of a larger society, and the actions of one individual, of one company, of religious sect or state or nation affect us all. Liberals embrace social programs because they feel society has a responsibility to help those who are less fortunate. Liberals embrace environmental protection because they agree that cheap gasoline today is not worth the price future generations will pay in pollution and loss of health and the unknown consequences of world-wide environmental upheaval. Liberals respect workers' rights because we know that each of us has equal right to a living wage, a roof over our heads, and healthcare for ourselves and our children. Liberals are for the people, all of the people, and do what they can to help each other and society at large, not because it makes them money, but because it is simply the right and fair thing to do.

So, is John Kerry a Liberal? His voting record shows him to be certainly far more liberal than Bush and Company. But in an election year, he can't admit to it. And that is a damn shame. Because the qualities that make a liberal – acceptance of others, a desire for equal treatment for all men and women, a sense of social responsibility – are qualities of which he should be proud.

America needs to remember what "liberal" really means. Every man and woman wants and deserves equal respect, dignity and justice. A liberal in the White House could help bring us closer to that. George W. Bush and his cronies, who think "Liberal" is an insult, never can.

One of the most powerful weapons the right uses, frequently and to great effect, is the distillation of complex issues to misleadingly simple arguments which bear a surface resemblence to logic, but which, once penetrated by analysis, are thin as paper and as logical as the plot of a soap opera. The fact that, beyond that initial glance, these arguments do not hold water is of little consequence, since few Americans are ever going to examine these arguments thoroughly, or even **try** to poke holes in them.

My favorite example of this (and a scary one, at that) is the classic "flat tax" argument, especially as espoused by Grover Norquist, an incredibly intelligent, reasoned and charismatic political machine. Boiled down to it's basics, Grover's argument is that the current progressive income tax structure is "unjust" because it treats people differently – that is, rich people pay a larger percentage of their income than poor people. A flat tax, he argues, is "just," because it treats all parties equally – all people (living beyond a certain threshold) pay an equal percentage of their wages (typical in this argument is 10% to 15%) in taxes.

At first consideration, this does seem logical. But the problem with crying that the tax code is unjust, and trying to level the playing field there, is that our wage system is unjust to begin with. If everyone were **paid** equally, according to effort, skill and quality of work, whatever that work, then it would make sense for everyone to be **taxed** equally. But, since the wage system is unjust (for example, a man working hard 80 hours a week at three minimum-wage jobs still makes far less than I do at 40 hours a week), a "just" flat tax system only further tilts the playing field in favor of those who hold large amounts of capital. Thus, Grover's argument has the surface appearance of logic, but with huge underlying flaws.

Spain, Terror and the War in Iraq

David Nett   March 18, 2004

There's a line of thought rolling through the conservative media this week that goes a little something like this:

Spain's new leader says the war in Iraq had nothing to do with the "War on Terror." Yet Spain posits that the recent commuter bombing of 3/11, whose perpetrators may be terrorists with ties to Al Qaeda, could be a result of Spain's participation in the Iraq war. Therefore, Spain is contradicting itself – if the war in Iraq wasn't about terror, then how could the resulting terror be about the war in Iraq?

Conclusion: Spain is acting illogically.

Thing is, it's this conservative message that is illogical, or, more correctly, it's a sort of "false logic" similar to what Max Shulman might have called "Post Hoc." According to these conservatives, if we assume that the terrorist attack against Spain was a result of its participation in the Iraqi War, then the Iraqi War must have been about terrorism. This has the surface appearance of logic, but, while both items are linked through the Iraqi War, they do not have the direct cause/effect relationship characterized by these conservative pundits. This can be shown fairly easily, by examining the Spanish positions that the conservatives find contradictory:

Statement 1: The U.S.-led war in Iraq had nothing to do with terrorism.

The past year has moved us closer to proving definitively that this statement is true. The American people were duped into believing that Iraq had weapons of mass destruction and was capable and even likely of giving or selling them to Islamic terrorist groups with whom Saddam had close ties, including (as was reported) Al Qaeda. It turns out, after a year of digging and probing, that not only did Iraq *not* have these weapons or even real weapon programs, they had no significant ties with any Islamic terrorists (Iraq was, after all, a secular dictatorship), and Saddam's name was (by many reliable reports) high on Al Qaeda's "hit list." So, while many of us (the American people and our elected officials), armed with incorrect or incomplete information, initially may have believed (say, in October of 2002) that an Iraqi war would be about terrorism, it was in fact waged for either entirely different, less public motives, or waged under false motives. In the end, the war had nothing to do with terrorism.

Statement 2: The 3/11 terrorist train bombing in Spain is a result of Spain's participation in the war in Iraq.

A stated goal of Al Qaeda, and, indeed, many other Islamic terrorist groups, is to rid the Middle East, viewed by these groups as a sacred Muslim homeland, of corrupting Western presence and influence. While the war in Iraq and the toppling of Saddam Hussein did nothing to directly negatively impact these terrorist groups (in fact, the chaos of war and the resulting social and economic consequences of postwar occupation have likely increased terrorist recruiting in the region, and have certainly provided increased opportunity for terrorist activity), the Western intrusion and subsequent occupation of "Arab" territory does go to the heart of Al Qaeda's argument for terrorism. Therefore, an act of terrorism against a participant in the war in Iraq is perfectly in line with Al Qaeda's normal operating procedures (and those of other Islamic terrorist groups).

It is therefore perfectly logical to state that, while the U.S.-led war in Iraq had nothing to do with fighting terrorism, a subsequent terrorist action against a participant in that war could well be a result of that same war and the resulting occupation. Spain's two "statements," while related through the inclusion of the War in Iraq as a central point of each, are not, as the conservatives have stated, contradictory or illogical.

Now, just because Spain's statement about the probable cause of the 3/11 bombing, however the conservatives spin it, is perfectly logical, that does not mean that it is true. Truth and logic are often different beasts, especially when dealing with complex human personal and political interactions (my wife, for instance, loves ketchup, but hates tomatoes – I ask you, is that logical?). The true, factual motives for the terrorist tragedy of 3/11 can be known only after extensive investigation into the incident, if they are ever known at all.

But painting Spain's new prime minister as "illogical" is blatantly wrong. As Dobie Gillis might have said, these conservative ideologues' "lack of information [is] terrifying. Nor would it be enough merely to supply [them] with information. First [they have] to be taught to 'think.'"

Iraq: One Year Later

Craig Bridger   March 22, 2004

So this is supposed to be a humorous website, but as we mark the one year anniversary of the official start of the Iraq war, I can't think of anything funny to say. One year ago, the Bush administration, flouting the will of the world, circumventing the United Nations, and reversing 50 years of American foreign policy, launched its illegal war of choice. One year ago, the fires of war were kindled with cherry-picked (sometimes entirely fabricated) "evidence" of weapons of mass destruction, stoked by rabid neo-conservative ideologues and fanned by a dishonest PR campaign – a dizzying spin job resembling nothing so much as a giant psychological game of three card monty – implying Saddam Hussein was responsible for 9/11. Now, one year later, those terrifying "weapons of mass destruction" have been down-graded to "weapons of mass destruction-related-activities," (or, in layman's terms, "my dog ate my homework"), our troops are greeted daily with improvised explosions instead of roses, and our credibility in the world is harder to find than Uganda's contribution to the Coalition of the Willing. A lot has happened in a year. It's a heck of an anniversary. It's a dandy, my granddad would say.

I've thought a lot about how to mark this occasion and it seems fitting, since anniversaries are represented by numbers, to start with some:

- American casualties in Iraq: 572 (432 since May 1st - "Mission Accomplished")

- Americans wounded in Iraq: 3,254

- Coalition casualties in Iraq: 101

- Iraqi Military Casualties: 4,895 to 6,370 (estimated)

- Iraqi Civilian Casualties: 8,581 to 10,430 (estimated)

- American Troops in Iraq: 130,000

- Current Estimated Cost of the War: $107,040,475,999

While the administration congratulates itself on the liberation, violence in Iraq continues with terrible, numbing regularity. On Thursday, a suicide car bombing near a hotel in Basra killed two men and a boy. 15 people were wounded in the blast. On Wednesday, a powerful car bomb devastated the Mount Lebanon Hotel in central Baghdad, killing 7 (although this number is still disputed) and wounding 35. In one report on the BBC, a weeping Iraqi man pled to the camera. "If this is liberation," the translator's voice deadpanned, "we don't want it."

Elsewhere in the world, high-ranking members of Pakistan's government (including Abdul Qadeer Khan, the "father" of the Pakistani atomic bomb) have been implicated in a nuclear black market that sold plans and parts to Libya, Iran, and North Korea, among others. Mohamed ElBaradei, head of the IAEA, called the Pakistani operation a "Wal-Mart" of nuclear technology. It's also been called the most threatening activity of proliferation in history. Proliferation. Precisely what the "Bush Doctrine" hoped to prevent with its policy of unilateral, pre-emptive wars. Weapons of mass destruction, anyone?

In Madrid, the death toll from last week's horrific bombings stands at 201.

I just went online to check a fact for this piece and saw the following on Yahoo: *Insurgents Kill Two Marines in Iraq*. I can't keep up with the tragedies. My statistics are already outdated and I haven't even finished the first draft of this thing. But here's the point. Howard Dean was lambasted in the "liberal" media for asking this question, but how exactly – more than 3 months after capturing one smelly old man in a hole – have we made the world any safer?

But perhaps the most troubling thing about the whole situation is this administration's brazen disregard for the truth. They don't even try to hide the fact that they're lying to us. And they're not even new lies. They're the same old lies that have already been thoroughly discredited. That's how much they think of us. They can't be bothered to invent less obvious falsehoods.

Since mainstream media often doesn't seem interested in the job, let me show you how easy it is to play a little game called "Investigative Journalism," also known as "Google." In fact, you don't even need Google anymore. U.S. Representative Henry Waxman has done all the work for you. His office has just released a document called *The Iraq on the Record* report, which is, to quote the report: "a comprehensive examination of the statements made by the five Administration officials most responsible for providing public information and shaping public opinion on Iraq: President George W. Bush, Vice President Richard Cheney, Defense Secretary Donald Rumsfeld, Secretary of State Colin Powell, and National Security Advisor Condoleezza Rice." The report identifies 237 different misleading statements made by these five individuals in the months before the war, and immediately after its commencement. It's also a searchable database. Let the fun begin.

Here's Rumsfeld on Face the Nation last weekend:

Schieffer: "Well, let me just ask you this. If they did not have these weapons of mass destruction, though...why then did they pose an immediate threat to us, to this country?"

Sec. Rumsfeld: "Well, you're the – you and a few other critics are the only people I've heard use the phrase "immediate threat." I didn't. The president didn't. And it's become kind of folklore that that's – that that's what's happened."

Now, here's Rumsfeld, in testimony to the Senate Armed Services Committee on 9/19/02, courtesy of Waxman's report:

"No Terrorist state poses a greater or more **immediate threat** to the security of our people than the regime of Saddam Hussein and Iraq." (bold font mine)

Wow. Moveon.org scooped me on that (and God bless them for it) but it's worth revisiting here, just to remind ourselves how little regard the Secretary has for the truth. In fact, that's what I'd call a double lie. There's his original lie, that Iraq posed an immediate threat to the United States, coupled with his new, more baffling lie, that he never said that – that it's all "folklore."

And here's President Bush, who has also suggested that the press concocted the idea that Iraq was an imminent threat:

"On its present course, the Iraqi regime is a threat of unique urgency...it has developed weapons of mass death."

But my favorite quote on this subject is this one, from our very own

Condeleezza Rice:

"The problem here is that there will always be some uncertainty about how quickly he can acquire nuclear weapons. But we don't want the smoking gun to be a mushroom cloud."

I'd say a nuclear bomb detonating inside the United States is a pretty goddamn immediate threat, wouldn't you, Don?

Rumsfeld, by the way, continues to insist that we will find weapons of mass destruction in Iraq. This, despite the fact that the administration's own handpicked inspector, David Kay, resigned in frustration in January, saying: "We were wrong." I guess Saddam wanted to stockpile all of those tons of botchulism and anthrax and mustard gas so that he could *hide* them in a secret place when his country was *invaded*. And Cheney, only a couple months ago, was still rolling out that old whopper about a clandestine meeting between Iraqi secret agents and Mohammed Atta before September 11th.

Now, perhaps the administration is so morally bankrupt that they will say anything to promote it's imperialist, war-profiteering agenda, which would make them truly Machiavelli's progeny, or they really believe this stuff, in which case they're just deranged. As Riggs says to Murtaugh, "Either way, I'm fucked." Or, as our fearless leader told Diane Sawyer when asked about the deception in stating that there were weapons of mass destruction, as opposed to the possibility that Iraq could move to acquire them:

"So, what the difference?"

Anyway, Angola, Azerbaijan, Eritrea, Estonia, Ethiopia, Micronesia, Rwanda, Slovakia, and Uzbekistan, Happy Anniversary. Thanks for being part of the best darn coalition anywhere. Don't worry about Germany or France ... or Poland ... or those socialist-nancy-boy-appeasers in Spain. We know who our real allies are. Palau, Macedonia, way to go. Let's all look forward to another upcoming anniversary, November of 2004, which I will celebrate by helping my fellow Americans elect a president. And this time, the guy with the most votes goes to Pennsylvania Avenue.

Condi, Disrespect and the 9/11 Families

Jeanette Scherrer   April 12, 2004

I actually set my alarm and got up to watch the live testimony of Condoleezza Rice to the 9/11 panel. I even made myself eggs, sausage and coffee. Now, you have to understand, for me to get up at 6AM for anything is nothing short of a miracle.

One thing I quickly came away with was that Dr. Rice is undeniably a very intelligent, accomplished woman. She was measured, smart and unflappable in her answers. She said there was no "silver bullet" that would have stopped the 9/11 attacks. She very subtly placed blame on the Clinton administration and Richard Clarke. She kept saying that the memos she received were not actionable. That's one that bothered me. She received, many from Richard Clark, memos, e-mails and/or PDBs (Presidential Daily Briefings) that talked about terrorism. Some said Al Qaeda cells were in the U.S., one said that Middle Eastern men were at U.S. flight schools learning how to fly large planes but weren't so concerned about landing them, one PBD, on Aug 6, 2001, was titled "Bin Laden Determined to Attack Inside the United States." Now that one was interesting. Apparently Dr. Rice dismissed this PDB as not containing anything relevant or of great importance, but yet continues to refuse to declassify it, as the administration has refused to declassify almost 10,000 documents. My real problems were not necessarily what she said, which was predictable, but with the issues surrounding these hearings.

First of all, the Bush administration refused to even have a commission until the families of 9/11 kept pushing for one. If they hadn't done that, there would be no investigation, none, into the worst terrorist attack on American soil. How is that it's okay to spend millions of dollars to determine whether Clinton did or did not lie about a blow job, but not okay to investigate an obvious breakdown and failure of intelligence that resulted in 9/11? You can't tell me that along the way somebody or "sombodies" didn't drop the ball and should be forced to take responsibility. 9/11 doesn't warrant an investigation? So after stonewalling and dragging their feet, Bush appoints

Henry Kissinger to head the commission. Are you fucking kidding me? I won't get into the problems with that, but please do your own research into Kissinger. Finally, a commission was appointed, one that was supposed to be non-partisan, which brings up another problem. I watched Thursday as the Republicans, in obvious partisanship, lobbed soft, squishy questions to Dr. Rice. The questions got much more pointed and tough with the Democratic commission members. So I question the validity of the panel in the first place.

Another problem is that when Bush was told of the attacks, he continued to sit in a Florida school classroom. In fact, he sat in there for almost five minutes after he was told the second plane hit. I was home with a badly sprained ankle, sleeping, when my best friend called me from Missouri to wake me up, and I ran to the television. But Bush just sat there. Then he and everyone else went and hid in a hole, while Richard Clarke stayed in the White House trying to figure out what happened and what we should do. The same Richard Clarke, I might add, who apparently "wasn't in the loop." Why didn't the Bush administration want a commission? The obvious question is what do they have to hide? In his new book, *Worse Than Watergate*, John Dean, Richard Nixon's lawyer, says that the Bush administration is more secretive than the Nixon administration. Now that's saying something. This White House, if they could, would choose to operate in total secrecy. One of the reasons they didn't want a 9/11 commission is because they feel they are above the checks and balances system. They, who are public servants by the way, would prefer to operate in total secrecy. They, especially Cheney, believe the loss of secrecy is eroding presidential power. He even disagreed with the investigation into Iran-Contra. And this from Bush, "I have an obligation to make sure that the presidency remains robust and that the legislative branch doesn't end up running the executive branch." To steal from John Dean, "secrecy is the way if dictatorships, not democracies."

Could the 9/11 attacks have been stopped? I really don't know. But what needs to be stopped is this administration, which has said a big, fat "fuck you" to the families of 9/11 and an even bigger "fuck you" to the American people from day one.

In the spring of 2004, I sent an email to all of the CSP contributors, letting them know that this would be the year, should any of them be so inclined, to really get their political views out to the public. With the war in Iraq and the presidential campaign in full swing, traffic to our political essays was increasing, but I was not certain that would last beyond November's election.

The next day Eli sent this piece. It's my favorite of all the political essays on CSP. Eli's not an overtly political guy, but this simple, silly essay is as clever and beautiful an outcry against discrimination as I've ever read.

Mothmen: A Solution

Eli Chartkoff   April 19, 2004

I am a mothman, and I am not exposed of extinction as supposed.

I want to be able to live where you do, and the companion with whom I want. I want to be able to drive your cars and to eat your food.

Is this evil? Why is this erroneous? Why can you say to me? Years ago I went to a place where I lived in a box close to a sump. The box had a terrible odor. Why is it? It is because it is your defect.

You are bad people. Soon because of our inexpensive labour market you will be demolished. You will be a race of private apes. You will be sorry then as we carry your coffee drinks of slat and pour them on our shoes. As we laugh. As we dance. Soon!

I am covered in fine hairs and can fly. I have a Proboscis, which ripples itself/crinkles. I date your daughter. I am a mothman!

Sincere,

A Mothman

In April of 2004, my sister Jaime told me over the phone that she thought she could convince Mom to vote for John Kerry. This intrigued me – I'd more or less written-off my parents, as far as politics went. They were long-time Republican voters, smack in the middle of a deeply Republican state (at least so far as presidential politics are concerned). I was hoping to change other peoples' minds through my writing, but it never even occurred to me I might try this with my parents, especially with my Dad. I decided to give it a shot, and hopefully help change not only their minds, but the minds of other like-thinking folks as well.

I knew it would take more than just my opinion to sway them. Since they raised me to appreciate reason and logic, it seemed to me (at the time) that the primary political difference between them and me was likely a difference in the information we were getting. In order to change their minds, then, I'd have to provide them easy access to the same articles and essays I found compelling, to which they were unlikely to be exposed on their own. So, my arguments would be a combination of editorial by me, and links to other online articles, grouped thematically – those links actually being the more important portion.

Because of the nature of these pieces, and the importance of the links, translating them from the web to the page was akward. What I've done here is include the editorial portions as they were originally written, and, at the end of each, list as many of the originally referenced articles as are still viewable online as "further reading."

For the record, none of the writers or publications which are mentioned as "further reading" have endorsed or are in any way connected with this book. <END ASS-COVERING>

My Republican Dad: Election '04, Part 1

David Nett   April 22, 2004

As I've written before, I come from a long line of Republicans. My maternal grandfather was a Reaganite Conservative Republican in every sense, and on the North Dakota State Legislature. When I got an earring, every single male member of my family (except my Dad and his father) told me I'd ruined my future – that none of them would ever even consider hiring someone with an earring. Especially if it was in my right ear, because that meant I was gay.

Times have changed. My conservative grandfather has passed on. My Dad's parents have chilled decidedly, accepting my (and my siblings') defection from the Catholic Church and my sister's budding political activism (and waffling sexual preferences), and still loving and supporting all of us. While many of my aunts and uncles are still in varying states of religious right-wing denial, my parents and grandparents are increasingly socially liberal, and one of my favorite uncles is considering a run for state office as an independent (he won't run as a Republican anymore, but he won't embrace the Democratic party either). Years of university theater, gay roommates, same-sex partners and kids moving to California have now softened their perceptions of society and all of it's infinitely weird variations.

Yet, despite an increased social concern, both of my parents still vote Republican. I believe some of it is out of habit, tradition, and a misunderstanding of the modern Democratic party (and it's legacy of Progressive Liberalism – social reform and fiscal responsibility). I think what is really missing in the socially-accepting but fiscally-conservative American heartland is a true understanding of what has happened to the modern Republican party under Religious and Neocon stewardship.

It is my goal to change my parents' minds (and the minds of other one-time Republicans whose social conscience is too big to fit in the Neocons' nutshell) before the November election. Over the summer and into the fall, I'll be publishing these "political primers" – really, just collections of links to stories, articles and editorials that my parents and others like them might not otherwise see.

Look – I'm not some brilliant political scientist, obviously. What I know is a combination of what I read, see and hear, and what my brain extrapolates from that knowledge, just like my parents, and just like everyone else. These articles aren't a way to say "I'm smarter that you," or "my beliefs are right and yours are wrong." Rather, they're a way to say, "We believe more of the same things than you realize. Here are some things you might not have read, that may (hopefully) bring you to the conclusion that re-electing Bush is not the way to make our country better."

This first group of links deals with general election issues. More will come, dealing with Iraq, 9/11, the economy, social issues, the Bush legacy and more. This first batch comes entirely (by coincidence) from *Salon.com*.

Further Reading:

- *Republicans for Kerry* (M. Goldberg & P. Caffera, in *Salon.com*, 03.26.04)

- *Conservatives are Outraged – About Bush* (M. Goldberg, in *Salon.com*, 01.27.04)

- *Kerry vs. the Chickenhawks* (R. Poe, in *Salon.com*, 02.19.04)

- *Pinocchio Presidency* (J. Wilson, in *Salon.com*, 03.16.04)

- *The Secret History of Secrecy* (J. Podesta & J. Legum, in *Salon.com*, 03.22.04)

My Republican Dad: Election '04, Part 2

David Nett   May 17, 2004

C had and I are from the same small town in North Dakota. He recently sent me this email:

> "I finally read this thing [*ed. note: the Real L-Word*] you wrote for Clark Schpiell. I just wanted to bring up a point about the stigma surrounding the word Liberal. Republicans are [...] ruled by their purse strings. [...] And, I think, they've used the word Liberal to indicate liberal spending, which a lot of lower middle class people don't appreciate (not to mention a bunch of old rich white guys). Probably the only reason my dad's a Republican is that he doesn't like the way Democrats spend his money. He explained to me once that the reason [North Dakota] has Republican governors and Democratic congressmen is that we want Congress to send money our way, and we want the governor to keep it in the state. So, again, it's all about money."

Chad's right. "Moderate Republicans" or "Eisenhower Republicans," who I (and many others) believe are the vast majority of the Republican Party, are not religious wackos or war-mongers. They are regular folks who work hard to make their money, and want their tax dollars spent responsibly – not an unreasonable request. That's why one of the primary pillars of every Republican campaign is a tax cut, or a spending cut, a dig at the NEA (despite its infinitesimal budget), or an accusation that the "liberal" opponent wants to fund "expensive," and "unnecessary" social programs, will likely raise your taxes, and increase the budget deficit. In short, Republicans will save you money, Democrats will steal it from you.

It's an argument that's decades old. And, even if it ever was true (I'm not convinced it was), it's blatantly false now. Sure, Bush Jr. has cut taxes (by the way, you get a $300 tax break, while he and his ridiculously rich friends get a $60,000+ one), but spending has skyrocketed even as those "expensive, unnecessary" social programs have been cut, the deficit has ballooned to a size unheard of, and state and local tax increases (to make up for budget shortfalls caused in no small part by under-funded federal mandates) negate most, if not all, of the federal tax breaks for low and middle-income Americans. In short, Mr. Bush and team have not fulfilled the classic Republican promise of more money in your pocket. Unless, of course, you were very, very rich to begin with.

This second group of links deals with economic issues. More will come, dealing with Iraq, 9/11, social issues, the Bush legacy and more.

Further Reading:

- *Shell Game* (Chuck Collins, in *TomPaine.com*, 04.09.04)

- *Behind the Jobs Debacle* (James K. Galbraith, in *Salon.com*, 03.15.04)

- *Bush's Budget Lies* (Robert L. Borosage, in *the Nation*, 02.23.04)

- *The Bush Tax Increase* (Center for American Progress, 02.20.04)

- *Back to Basics* (Jonathan Tasini, in *TomPaine.com*, 03.15.04)

Farenheit 9/11: a Review

David Nett   June 28, 2004

*F*ahrenheit *9/11* is a movie for everyone, and I mean everyone, over the age of 15. Not everyone will like it, not everyone will agree with it, but everyone should see it.

For many people, *F9/11* will be a revelation – much of what is here are the sides of an almost four-year story that the mainstream media doesn't tell. They'll learn about the Bush administration's complicated relationship with the Middle East, and the Saudis in particular. They'll learn about Congress and the Patriot Act. They'll learn about what's going on in Iraq, in rural and small-town America in response to Iraq, what Homeland Defense and the War on Terror really mean, and who really has influence in issues of Defense, the State and International Affairs.

But, even for someone who keeps abreast of political and world issues, who reads the official and alternative versions of what's going on today, *F9/11* is an important film. Movies can crystallize ideas in ways that no book or article or blog can. In seeing what's going on, not in abstract, not in your mind's eye, but on-screen – real life, recorded in startling, furious color and sound – these ideas have a visceral impact. A film like this can take you from thinking an idea to really, truly feeling that idea; from intellectual acknowledgment to passion.

The importance of this movie aside, is it any good? The answer is, yes, absolutely. I'm a fan of Michael Moore's movies, and I think this might be the best of them (my previous favorite was *the Big One*, though they are all varying degrees of awesome). I think the reason is Moore's restraint – the subject matter in *F9/11* drives itself so well, and the emotion is so high, that Moore doesn't need to guide it, to provoke it, the way he has done in previous films. Unlike in *Bowling for Columbine* or *Roger & Me* or the *Big One*, Moore is behind the camera for the vast bulk of this film. There is much voice-over narrative, but he's seldom on screen. Frankly, for much of the film, his presence isn't needed – his pointing the camera in the right direction is enough.

F9/11 opens with election day in 2000, and spends some time with that most controversial transfer of power in our nation's history. He lingers just long enough on Bush's first eight months in office to remind us what was happening in that clumsy time, and then moves to 9/11/2001. With surprising deft, he balances a sincere compassion for the victims and their families with a very detailed (and damning) look at the relationship between the Bush family and administration and the Saudi royal family and the Bin Ladens. After 9/11 and the Saudi/Bush education, he moves onto the initial aftermath, and the invasion of Afghanistan. But where the film really takes off is with the examination of our build to war in Iraq, and Bush's transformation into a war president. Most powerful (and gut-wrenching) is the documentation of the effects of the Iraq war on the lives of regular people. Here, Moore as a character nearly disappears, and we are launched on an emotional white-water with an ex-marine, the mother of an Army volunteer, and others. Again, for many of us, nothing here is new, but seeing it laid so bare, so human, is startling and dreadful. Do not be surprised when the tears come.

Moore has become a mature and powerful editorialist (which, by the way, is what he is – not a "documentarian"), and his storytelling ability, especially when he's proving a point using such rich source material, is enviable. He's not without his faults – his examination of Bush and the Saudis, while a clearly important piece of the 9/11 and Iraq puzzle, is sometimes too dry, angry and almost too detailed, and throws off the movie's rhythm. And the "what was GWB thinking?" device, while a clever way to introduce the Saudi/Bin Ladin connection and the Bush team's history, seems sometimes overly malicious. The most damning moments, for Bush, are found in his own speech, or when a frustrated, disillusioned soldier calls him a fool. The "GWB thinking" bit feels just a little out of step with the mood of the rest of the film, and reaches a bit too far.

However, none of this detracts too greatly from the overall quality of F9/11. As I said, not everyone will agree with Moore's obvious position and opinions, but nearly everyone will be impassioned enough by them to at least engage in debate (for or against), and that's the ultimate aim of a film such as this – to get people involved, to get them to (in Moore's own words) "do something." Especially in an election year, when issues like women's rights and religious freedoms and social welfare and our international relationships perch precariously on a cliff's edge, a film like this is of extreme importance. But, even after November 2004 has come and gone, *Fahrenheit 9/11* will remain a damn fine movie, and an important piece of cinematic, and political, history.

Do yourself a favor: go see it, and take someone, maybe someone who might not have gone otherwise, with you.

In the summer of 2004, more and more evidence began to come to light suggesting that Sudanese government was supporting the budding genocide in Darfur. You didn't know that because the American media didn't seem to notice, or to care, despite the top-notch reporting (by African journalists) and solidity of the evidence. And why should we? Africa is full of poor people who can't buy our exports, at least not at full price. Plus, we're up to our eyeballs in Iraq (where the oil is, remember?), and we've pretty much flushed our international diplomatic influence down the drain, so we couldn't do much about it even if we wanted to.

The Bush administration is only the most recent to utterly ignore African strife, at least until public pressure makes it impossible to continue (as is currently, it seems, beginning to happen). Neglecting the people of Africa has practically been U.S. policy for decades (if not longer). Even when things were relatively good here, we turned our backs on Rwanda — why should Sudan get any better treatment?

So, from our government to your oppressed and dying people: "Suck it, Africa."

GWB: Shame on Sudan

David Nett   July 12, 2004

Good news, folks. After some hard thinkin,' a respected team of legal experts has de ... deter... determo ... figured out that the current sitchiashun in Darfur is not technically "Genocide."

How can you say that, sir? One ethnic group, apparently backed by the government, appears to be attempting the extermination of another ethnic group, resulting, so far, in over 10,000 deaths, and an estimated million people fleeing from their homes. How can you not call that Genocide?

Well ... 'cause then we'd hafta do something. And there's no darn oil ., er .. liberation in there worth fightin' for.

Actually, sir, according to many sources, oil *has* recently been discovered in the Darfur region.

Then I'd just like to say to the Sudanese guv'ment: You have 24 hours to prove you have no Weapons of Mass Destruction...

My *Conservative* Dad: Election '04, Part 3

David Nett   June 21, 2004

A little while ago, I had a rare political discussion with my Dad via email. It was initiated by the first two "Republican Dad" articles, which made me extraordinarily happy – my first goal was simply to get my Dad (and others) to read this stuff.

Dad had many interesting and compelling things to say, the most striking of which was this:

> "Politically, I am basically conservative, but do not limit myself to the credo nor preachings of any party. I do not consider myself a 'sheep' who would mindlessly follow with the rest of the 'flock.' And herein lies the problem with the majority of the voting public. They chose from the 'political flavor of the month shepherd' offerings and then as good sheep do, simply follow blindly where the shepherd may wander according to what the media decides to let them hear."

I hear what Dad is saying – I'm a registered Democrat, but few are more pissed than I about my party's abandonment of the Progressive ideal in favor of corporate dollars and "appealing to the center." What's more, his comments about "following blindly ... what the media decides" are exactly what I'm trying to counter with these articles – I hope to show a side of the debate that may not normally be seen by my target audience, so they can make decisions armed with more, varied information. Anyway, what Dad said is exactly what I was counting on: Dad is one of the smartest (perhaps the smartest), most independent-minded men I know, and because of that, I have hope to sway his vote away from George W. Bush in November's election. He's stubborn, and sometimes set in his ways, but if he were a Republican party shill I wouldn't have bothered. It's because I know he's a rational, logical person with his own mind that I'm even writing these articles. Here's hoping your dad is the same.

So, we move from the mis-named "My Republican Dad" to the more appropriate "My Conservative Dad." And in this issue, I wanna take a short look at the War in Iraq. I was saving this for later in the summer, and I may focus on it again in the future. But I heard something late this week on NPR that startled and angered me. After the horrific beheading of American contractor Paul Johnson in Saudi Arabia, one of NPR's commentators said that Bush's approval ratings will likely get a four to five point bounce as a show of support for his "War on Terror" in Iraq. Upon hearing this, I pounded on my steering wheel, shouting and honking and gesturing wildly – surely the folks in neighboring cars heading south on the 101 must have thought I was an epileptic. But what I was screaming is this: If Bush had not launched his poorly planned War and Occupation of Choice in Iraq, Paul Johnson would still be alive today. It is as simple as that. Yes, terrorism would have continued to be a threat, with or without the war. Yes, an international "War on Terrorism" is an important part of the fabric of our world (newsflash: it was so before 9/11 in most of the world – we just didn't care). Yes, the war is a complicated matter, and our relationship with the nations of the middle-east is informed by complex, nuanced layers of political, ideological and economic realities, about which precious few in our nation are experts. But it is clear our war in Iraq was willful, unnecessary, and ill-planned, and these acts of terrorism, of murder, against us and against our allies are a direct result of that arrogant, unnecessary war and the chaotic and bloody occupation that continues today. It's not a statement you're likely to hear on the radio, or see on TV, but I firmly believe it is true. If it weren't for Bush's war, Paul Johnson would be alive today, and his death should not encourage support for Bush and his administration. I condemn the terrorists – they should be hunted down (these particular guys have been, though too late) and charged with a host of crimes. But we cannot pretend that our administration's arrogance, bloodthirstiness, and ultimate incompetence did not play a great part in these terrible events.

More thoughts on Iraq (I've included more op-ed columns than in previous *Dad* articles, but I think informed opinion is important here.):

Further Reading:

- *The New Pentagon Papers* (Karen Kwiatkowski, in *Salon.com*, 03.10.04)

- *Hiding War's Toll* (Nancy Lessin, in *Common Dreams*, 03.05.04)

- *Dark Victory* (Dr. Jeffrey Record, an exerpt from *Dark Victory*, 04.29.04)

- *At the Breaking Point* (Robert Schlesinger, in *Salon.com*, 04.29.04)

- *Clarke's Vindication* (David Sirota, in *Salon.com*, 04.20.04)

- *Swatting Flies* (Husain Haqqani, in *Salon.com*, 04.14.04)

- *What Do We Do Now?* (Howard Zinn, in *the Progressive*, 06.04)

- *10 Mistakes* (General Anthony Zinni, in *Salon.com*, 05.26.04)

- *Iraq on the Record* (Rep. Henry Waxman, 03.04)

My Conservative Dad: Election '04, Part 4

David Nett   September 9, 2004

I t's a little more than seven weeks until we, as a nation, decide who we want (or, for many of us, don't want) as President of the United States.

A lot of noise is being made right now about the mechanics of the election – paperless electronic voting versus electronic voting with printed confirmation, punch voting versus "connect the arrow" (can you believe, by the way, that the election coordinator who designed the infamous Florida "butterfly ballot" still has her job, and has designed yet another ballot for the same county for this election?), in-person voting versus absentee. And yet, whatever the noise, the issue at the center is crucial, and the same as it ever was – who do you want as your president?

Central also are the issues (though you'd never know it to watch the media coverage, obsessed only with character assassination): the economy, the war in Iraq, the "War on Terror," Social Security, Medicare, health insurance, women's rights, gay rights, the environment, and the list goes on and on. Chances are, neither major candidate (nor any of the minor ones) holds your same position on all of those issues. However, that is no reason to simply throw your hands in the air and not vote. This election is crucial to the future of the United States in the world, and the future of all her people. The numbers of poor and working poor are rapidly growing, the middle class is dwindling, the elderly are losing their benefits, reproductive rights are draining away, the environmental protections Clinton fought for are all but eviscerated and the United States, as an entity, is reviled in the world as never before. The economy is improving, but only if you are a corporation or an owner of large capital – the typical working person's income has actually dropped some $1,500 in the past few years.

Secluded here in Los Angeles, I've been hard-pressed to believe that there is anyone in this country who doesn't see the massive failings of the Bush administration as I do – when every single person with whom I come into contact is as disappointed in this presidency as I am, it is a startling thing to look at the polls and see a slight Bush lead. But my trip to the Midwest this past week brought a clearer picture for me. After seeing a few of the "swing state" ads, after hearing regular people, many of whom are out of work or are slaving below the poverty line, speak with affection about Bush, or at least bewilderment about Kerry, who they see as soft, an "intellectual" and, incredibly, a liar (hello, pot, this is kettle), I am less certain of a Kerry victory that I was a week ago. It seems incredible to me, but about half the country still really digs GWB.

I'm certain another week or so back in L.A. will shore up my confidence. In the meantime, please read these articles, and visit both the Kerry and the Bush campaign websites. And, for goodness sake, if you are in a swing state and are subject to the relentless attack ads (from both sides), visit FactCheck.org, so you can sort out the lies from the truth. Find out what is really going on in this country, how this administration is screwing regular folks, how an "ownership society" is really code for "screw the labor force."

I'll be back with more focused debate soon.

The articles here deal with the long-lasting legacy (read: stain) the first George W. Bush administration is likely to leave on the tapestry of American history, law and society, and what a second term might bring:

Further Reading:

- *And You Thought His First Term Was a Nightmare* (Charles Tiefer, in *Salon.com*, 08.25.04)

- *the Statement* (Diplomats and Military Commanders for Change, 06.16.04)

- *Who Pays And How* (Robert B. Reich, in *TomPaine.com*, 08.18.04)

- *Humiliated, Angry, Ashamed, Brown* (Ian Spiers, an Artist Essay, 2004)

- *the New Caesars* (Gary Hart, in *Salon.com*, 08.18.04)

- *Copyrighting the President* (Lawrence Lessig, *WIRED*, 08.04)

- *'Data Quality' Law Is Nemesis Of Regulation* (Rick Weiss, in the *Washington Post*, 08.16.04)

My Conservative Dad: Election '04, Part 5

David Nett   September 16, 2004

M ost Americans live paycheck to paycheck. A minority of us, myself included, are able to squirrel away a hundred bucks here and there and create a modest savings (that is all but wiped out any time there is an emergency, like a major auto breakdown or Christmas), but are still very much living for that bi-weekly check. A very small minority of us have enough extra cash, enough savings, enough "capital," that the income from those non-wage sources contributes significantly to our bottom line.

When George Bush touts his proposed second-term "ownership society," what he doesn't tell you is that regular people, those of us who live paycheck to paycheck, those of us for whom saving, especially in any significant amount, is a pipe dream, don't have a place in that ownership society. While removing tax burdens from savings accounts (whether for personal or medical or Social Security purposes) seems an intriguing proposition, it is all built on an assumption that, when bills are paid, you've got enough left over to contribute significantly to those tax-free accounts. For the 43+ million Americans who do not have health care, for instance, because they can't afford the $100 - $300 per month for base-line HMO coverage, what good is a tax-free savings account? Those folks are not buying health insurance because they can't afford – how can they afford to save $300 a month, even tax free, if they can't afford to spend $300 a month on health insurance?

Bottom line: we live in an America where most of us are scraping to get by. Those of us who are fortunate enough find ourselves in the dwindling "middle class" are desperately trying to keep ourselves there – sixty-hour work-weeks, no pensions, piddly savings, constant fear of job loss. This is not an America where a second-income is a source of extra money for a married couple, this is a world where that second income is a necessity to keep the bills, the mortgage, the school loans, out of default. The many millions of Americans who are working 40 or more hours each week and still riding below the poverty line (believe it, baby: the federal minimum wage at 40 hours per week amounts to less than $12000 per year, while the national average poverty line is around $15000), not to mention those who cannot work, or cannot find jobs in this "jobless recovery," aren't included in Bush's bold "ownership society." This administration's plans for our future economy are a fraud that no hard-working American should accept.

This group of articles highlight economic issues, and the Bush administration's inability to deal with, or outright exacerbation, of them:

Further Reading:

- *Taxes for an Ownership Society* by the Editorial Staff (in the *New York Times*, 09.15.04)

- *Why conservatives must not vote for Bush* by Doug Bandow (in *Salon.com*, 09.10.04)

- *The Truth About Job Numbers* by Robert Reich (in *TomPaine.com*, 09.09.04)

- *Bush's Game of Risk* by Harold Meyerson (in the *Washington Post*, 09.08.04)

- *The Slow Road Down* by Heather Boushey (in *TomPaine.com*, 08.27.04)

- *The Department of Labor's Final Overtime Regulations* by Ross Eisenbrey (in *Epinet*, 05.04.04)

- *America's hidden issue of poverty* by Robert Kuttner (in the *Boston Globe*, 06.16.04)

- *Sabotaging The Poor* by Deborah Cutler-Ortiz (in *TomPaine.com*, 06.29.04)

- *Milking The Middle Class* by Fernando Ferrer (in *TomPaine.com*, 09.16.04)

My Conservative Dad: Election '04, Part 6

David Nett   September 30, 2004

World government is not "going to happen." It *is* happening, right now – in a multitude of ways, the world is coming together, for better or for worse. As the European Union grows, and comes more completely together (as it does daily), it will shortly become the world's second, and perhaps primary, superpower. The International Monetary Fund and the World Trade Organization, separately, are weaving together the world's monetary interest into a single economic entity. The Kyoto treaty is attempting to wrap it's arms around global environmental damage, and the International Criminal Court around international atrocity. And, whether we want to acknowledge it or not, the United Nations is the focal point for almost all international exchange.

We're standing on the outside of this, in almost every instance. The EU governs itself, the IMF and WTO are governed primarily by corporate greed (this is the one area in which we are most involved, through our corporations). We refused Kyoto. We refused the ICC. We treat the United Nations with disrespect and contempt, unless politeness suits our purpose. The U.S., it seems, especially under the current administration, wants no part in world governance, unless "world governance" means "the rest of y'all do what we tell ya to do." As a result, we are being passed over. Passed by. Because we insist that the only role we want to play is that of ruler, we've begun to lose our voice, our potential for input and real leadership, in the global arena. I'd argue that, right now, the only thing keeping us on the table is the pure muscle of our huge economy and military might. We are the rich bully – the "Blaine," if you will (for *Pretty in Pink* fans) – of international affairs. We're invited to the party 'cause we've got the cash and the body, even though the world knows we're unlikely to come, and, if we do show up, we're more likely to pick a fight than to add to the conversation.

Our current president cannot, and, in fact, is unwilling at a fundamental level, to fix this. His stubbornness, arrogance, and disregard for the people of the world in general will not allow it. John Kerry may not be able to fix this, either – after the past four years especially, it is a monumental task. But at least he appears willing to try. I think, with our support, he may succeed.

Tonight brings us the first presidential debate. The subject is foreign policy, and will hinge primarily on Iraq and the War on Terror, certainly. Iraq represents more than just a war in the Middle East during this election. Iraq represents:

- deception on the part of this administration

- disregard for the opinions of the American people

- disregard for the opinions of the world population

- insensitivity to other cultures

- disregard for American lives in the face of political gain

- disregard for human life in general

- disregard for the studied opinions and, indeed, lives, of our military personnel

- lack of commitment to the actual declared "War on Terror"

- inability to admit error, and take corrective action

- the use of fear and intimidation to retain power

- a growing international anti-American sentiment

- disrespect for the UN and its members

- an inability for this administration to plan for the consequences of its actions

Since we're getting close, and this issue is so important, there's a lot of reading below. I encourage you to slog through all of it, if you can. What has happened with our war of choice in Iraq is almost beyond belief. It's our duty to learn about it and, whatever the outcome of this election (fingers crossed), make certain it does not happen again.

Further Reading:

- *Baghdad Year Zero* (Naomi Klein, *Harper's*, 09.24.04)

- *Match Iraq Policy to Reality* (Jessica Mathew, *Washington Post*, 09.23.04)

- *The bubble boy* (Sidney Blumenthal, *Salon.com*, 09.23.04)

- *Hell* (Phillip Robertson, *Salon.com*, 09.23.04)

- *Red Alert* (Matthew Brzezinski, *Mother Jones*, 09.04)

- *Bush's decisions defined by ideology* (Walter Williams, *Seattle Post-Intelligencer*, 09.28.04)

- *The Cowardly Broadcasting System* (Mary Jacoby, *Salon.com*, 09.29.04)

- *The Afghan effect?* (James K. Galbraith, *Salon.com*, 09.21.04)

- *Uncle Sam is hard at work for U.S. corporations* (Walter Williams, *Seattle Post-Intelligencer*, 09.27.04)

- *"Fantasy" clashes with reality over Iraq policy* (Mary Jacoby, *Salon.com*, 09.27.04)

- *Who Kills Hostages in Iraq?* (Samir Haddad and Mazin Ghazi, *Al Zawra*, , 09.19.04)

- *Turning point* (David J. Morris, *Salon.com*, 09.16.04)

- *The Opportunity Costs of the Iraq War* (Center for American Progress, 08.25.04)

- *How George Bush bankrupted the war on terror* (Farhad Manjoo, *Salon.com*, 09.11.04)

- *The unwinnable war* (James Carroll, *Boston Globe*, 09.07.04)

- *These Are Their Ends* (Patrick C. Doherty, *TomPaine.com*, 08.05.04)

- *Asserting This War Has Made Us Safer Won't Make It So* (Tom Maertens, *Common Dreams*, 07.27.04)

- *The Man Behind The Curtain* (John Prados, *TomPaine.com*, 07.19.04)

- *Corrupted Intelligence* (Ray McGovern, *TomPaine.com*, 07.12.04)

- *The Costs of Bush's War* (Katrina vanden Heuvel, *the Nation*, 06.29.04)

My Conservative Dad: Election '04, Part 7

David Nett   October 18, 2004

I've spoken more about politics with my Dad in the last four months than I probably have in my entire life. Interestingly, we both feel very much the same about where our system is broken, and how, and about how the "human nature factor," as I call it, prevents the implementation of any purely idealistic solution, whatever the socialists or free-marketeers might tell you. Our proposed solutions to this are pretty widely divergent, unfortunately.

I think this is the item which picks at me most, and which I didn't see as clearly when I began these articles. The fact is, presented with the same exact evidence, equally intelligent, reasonable people may come to many different conclusions, based upon who they are and their individual beliefs. These articles were meant to provide more of that "same information," so that we all were on the same page about our upcoming presidential election. In the end, as I've said, folks will make their choice based upon personal perception. But I still believe, especially for those whose minds are not set, consuming the stories and articles and surveys I've recommended can make a difference in swaying votes away from George W. Bush, and toward John Kerry. That is, presented with the "facts," such as we are able to determine them, voters who are not ideologically tied to one party or another will lean toward Kerry.

Another point of interest I've discovered in this process is how differently politics is portrayed in the news, depending upon where you reside in this country. Information with which I've been bombarded these past months in southern California seems to be barely a blip on the news in North Dakota. At the same time, shades of issues which seldom make our nightly news here have been getting large play there. In addition, surrounded by like-minded friends in a fairly liberal part of the country (we shouldn't take that for granted, however – currently, Kerry is ahead of Bush by a disturbingly narrow margin in California), I tend to take some of my political assertions for granted. In the last Conservative Dad article, I referenced Bush's "inability to admit error." My assumption was, based upon the readily available information about the economy, Iraq, etc., and Bush's own admission at a press conference a few months ago and going on since then that he "would do everything exactly the same" and that he "couldn't think of any errors" (loosely quoted), that everyone recognized this trait in the administration. My Dad's simple and telling response: "Here I must say I do not 'know' the errors that have been made, nor by whom they may have been made."

Fair enough. So, this second-to-last (as we are rapidly nearing November 2) *Conservative Dad* will take a slightly different format from previous installments. In this one, I'll highlight the handful of broad, major failings I see in this administration, illustrated by various external articles (some new, some already hi-lighted). Basically, this is a rundown, on a macro scale, of why I think you should not vote to re-elect George Bush (sit back – this will be a long one).

The War in Iraq:

Going into Iraq was a poor choice by our president. While our congress voted to grant him the power to use military force if necessary (a vote with which I disagreed), I believe that the President mislead our elected officials regarding his desire to find a peaceful solution, and to work in concert, if possible, with our traditional allies. In addition, the President and his administration, unhappy with the pre-war conclusions of our usual intelligence and military planning groups, created a new group in the Department Of Justice specifically charged with finding reasons to invade Iraq, and whose "intelligence" painted the rosiest of pictures about that potential invasion, and what we'd need to "win" a war there. Ignoring then the less sunny intelligence and estimates of our military commanders and other experts, the administration drew up a plan for war in Iraq which relied upon broad, unrealistic, idealistic suppositions: that the war would be a cakewalk, that the Iraqi people would welcome the invasion, that there would be little or no post-war insurgence, that we could do it "on the cheap" with few soldiers on the ground for only a very short period, and that we'd have a friendly, democratically-elected government installed within a year or so of the invasion. All this, whether or not we were supported by the international community at large. It was a bad idea from the start, and I (and millions of others) said so – we were dismissed as crazies. Of course the invasion itself went well – we are the most powerful military force in the world, with soldiers whose skills are unparalleled and hardware the envy of all other nations. Still, we did not secure important locations, or prevent looting and chaos. And, since the invasion, the Bush administration has continually painted a picture of Iraq far rosier than those on the ground are telling, has shrouded the homecoming of our fallen soldiers in secrecy (not to mention the fact that Bush has not attended a single soldier's funeral), has kept the numbers of wounded secret (or difficult to extract), has not even bothered to officially count the Iraqi dead (civilian or military), and has generally failed to "win the peace" – in fact, creating conditions which draw foreign fighters from across the borders, and create increasing hordes of local insurgents.

This is all important for three fundamental reasons:

- While we cannot go back and undo the way this war was conducted, understanding the fundamental failings shows us the enormously faulty process of decision-making in this administration.

- The administration's ongoing plan for the war is no more clear, nor more well-thought-out, than any of its initial plans, dooming us (and our brave troops) to years of continued conflict there. In creating such an unstable situation, a breeding-ground for terrorists, we have made the world more dangerous, not safer, as was the intention. Continuing without a major policy shift will make the world even more dangerous.

- This ill-planned, ill-executed war does not only cost us in the goodwill of the world and in the blood and lives of our troops, it costs us in a very fundamental way as it continues to drain much-needed funds from our economy, deepening our already gigantic debt, and increasing the burden of us and on future generations.

Further Reading:

- *The New Pentagon Papers* (Karen Kwiatkowski in *Salon.com*, 03.04)

- *Hiding War's Toll* (Nancy Lessin in *TomPaine.com*, 03.04)

- *Hell* (Phillip Robertson in *Salon.com*, 09.04)

- *Costs of Bush's War* (Katrina vanden Heuvel in *the Nation*, 06.04)

- *The Turning Point* (David J. Morris in *Salon.com*, 09.04)

The Economy:

While George W. Bush did not inherit a recession, as he claims (most economists point to March of 2001 as the beginning of the recession), he did inherit an economy down dramatically from its late-90's high point. However, his policies of reckless tax-cuts (aimed at entirely the wrong sector) and increased corporate welfare have exacerbated the problem, making way for our current so-called "jobless recovery." His continued disregard for the unemployed, the working poor and the struggling middle-class has created the largest income gap between the rich and the poor in our nation's modern history. Instead of addressing economic issues head-on, he pushes for permanent tax cuts, and touts underfunded education programs, despite the fact that even our college graduates are having increasing trouble finding jobs which pay above the wildly out-of-sync-with-cost-of-living minimum wage.

Further Reading:

- *Who Pays, And How* (Robert Reich in *TomPaine.com*, 08.04)

- *Bush's Budget Lies* (Robert L. Borosage in *the Nation*, 02.04)

- *The Bush Tax Increase* (Center for American Progress, 02.04)

- *Taxes for an Ownership Society* (*New York Times*, 09.04)

- *What Economic Recovery?* (James K. Galbraith in *Salon.com*, 10.04)

- *The Slow Road Down* (Heather Boushey in *TomPaine.com*, 08.04)

- *The Truth about Job Numbers* (Robert Reich in *TomPaine.com*, 09.04)

- *Conservatives Must Not Vote for Bush* (Doug Bandow in *Salon.com*, 09.04)

- *Sabotaging the Poor* (Deborah Cutler-Ortiz in *TomPaine.com*, 06.04)

- *Time to Commit* (Bernie Sanders in *In These Times*, 09.04)

Social Issues:

While all manner of "social issues" are at stake in this election, three large issues loom here, and all can be tied to a single point: Bush makes policy based entirely upon his religious views, regardless of the wider implications, or the prohibition of such actions under the First Amendment. Whether the issue is stem cell research, abortion, or gay marriage, the fundamental argument against these issues, the argument upon which this administration stands, is a religious one: the religion practiced by George W. Bush tells him these things are wrong and therefore they must be made illegal. Never mind our freedom to choose our own religious beliefs, which may contradict his. Never mind the lives which could be improved or even saved by any of these. His God tells him they are wrong, and we must all be subject to the perceived laws of his God, whatever we personally believe.

Public policy should not be completely dictated by personal religious fervor. Of course religion will factor into a president's personal conviction, and the fundamental teachings of his religion will color how he leads. But his beliefs should not be forced onto the population at large. Our Constitution specifically prohibits religious rule, and rightly so.

Further Reading:

- *War over Gay Marriage* (Tim Grieve in *Salon.com*, 02.04)

- *We're Not in Lake Wobegon Anymore* (Garrison Keillor in *In These Times*, 08.04)

- *Thou Shalt Not Make Scientific Progress* (Farhad Manjoo in *Salon.com*, 03.04)

- *Playing with Fire* (James Carroll in *TomPaine.com*, 03.04)

- *How George Bush Will Ban Abortion* (Michelle Goldberg in *Salon.com*, 10.03)

- *Why Can't this Nation Back Stem Cell Research?* (Mark Zimmerman in the *Baltimore Chronicle*, 10.04)

The Environment:

Simply put, Bush is no friend of the environment. He has systematically undone most of the environmental protections the Clinton administration won, whether by cutting funding, slashing enforcement, or simply cutting the programs outright. His "Healthy Forests" plan is a mockery of the Forest Service's recommendation for undergrowth and small-tree thinning, and his "Clear Skies" plan is a fundamental step backward from our existing Clean Air Act. His close personal relationship with the fossil fuel industry (coal and oil, especially) perpetuates a dangerous trend toward pollution rather than away from it, and causes him and his to ignore global warming entirely. His lip-service to a "hydrogen highway" (an imaginative but thoroughly impractical plan which, even if properly funded and effective, provides a possible solution that is 20 - 30 or more years away) totally ignores the pressing environmental (and economical) issues faced *right now* by our dependence on oil as our primary source of energy. To put it bluntly, Bush is tied too tightly to big corporate energy and chemical interests to give a crap about the environment.

Further reading:

- *A-pillaging We Will Go* (Katharine Mieszkowski in *Salon.com*, 06.04)

- *Dirty Secrets* (Osha Gray Davidson in *Mother Jones*, 09.03)

- *Does George Bush Know What Science Is?* (Katharine Mieszkowski in *Salon.com*, 09.04)

- *Global Warming is Just Hot Air* (Katharine Mieszkowski in *Salon.com*, 09.04)

- *Bush Declares War on Environment* (Bill Press in *Inside Politics*, 03.01)

- *Crimes Against Nature* (Robert F. Kennedy Jr. and Jeff Fleischer in *Mother Jones*, 10.04)

These are just the broad assessments. For more (much, much more), you should visit *One Thousand Reasons* (www.thousandreasons.net), a smashing website documenting the "failures of the Bush administration."

Next week: Why you should vote *for* John Kerry.

My Conservative Dad: Election '04, Part 8

David Nett   October 28, 2004

Sure, you've been saying these past months, it's easy to kick Bush around, to spout tens, hundreds, thousands of reasons why we shouldn't vote for him. But, you say, perhaps you should tell us why we should vote *for* John Kerry.

Okay, this is another long one:

Reason 1:

John Kerry appears to be a thoughtful man. That is not to say he's polite, and uses frequent "pleases" and "thank-yous" (though I'm sure that is the case). What I mean to say is that, when presented with a problem, he pursues information about that problem and, based upon available information, he determines a best course of action. When not enough information is available, he delays decision while he (or his aides) investigate further. What's more, after having made a decision, he continues to review incoming relevant information, and is not afraid to re-shape his decision based upon this new information. That is, it is more important for him to be as right as he can be, given all the information, than to have been right in the first place.

What's more, Kerry is capable of complex consideration, of weighing the various shades of gray of an issue and attempting to find the best possible of many sometimes undesirable solutions. Take, for example, Kerry's voting on the $87 billion supplemental budget grant for the war in Iraq. Kerry voted in favor of a version of the bill which granted the $87 billion, but required congress to find a way to pay for it from the current fiscal budget, partially by rolling back much of the top-tier of Bush's vaunted tax cuts. He agreed the funds were necessary for a successful prosecution of the war, and he also believed that, since the congress and administration had committed us to war, it was their responsibility to find a way to finance it. That version of the bill was scrapped. A subsequent version granted the same amount of funds, but, instead of planning to pay for it in the short term, this second version of the bill simply added it to the deficit, leaving its payment to future generations. That refusal of responsibility, coupled with a realization that there was to be little or no oversight in the spending of the $87 billion, caused Kerry to vote against this second version, despite the fact he believed the money was necessary. It was a vote of futility – the bill was guaranteed to pass – but it was a vote of conscience against those who would wage war without consideration for who would pay the inherent costs.

That is the kind of reasoned thinking I was raised to respect. It's the way my Ma and Pa (as much as humans raising four smartass kids can) thought, it's the way my most respected instructors in high school and college thought. I was raised to respect intelligent, thoughtful reasoning, and I do.

Not everyone does. Hence the idea of Kerry the "Flip-Flopper." There are lots of folks who look at Kerry and say, "he doesn't stick to his decisions." They see him vote for giving Bush the power to go to war (a vote with which I disagree, but understand and respect the motive), then against the $87 billion, and think "the guy wanted to go to war, now he doesn't want to pay for it," which is exactly the opposite of the truth. Kerry did not want to go to war, but he wanted the president to be empowered with the ultimate bargaining chip. Kerry wanted the president to use diplomacy to further contain Iraq, and to force Iraq to accept weapons inspectors (which, ultimately, they did, though the inspectors were not given time enough to complete their jobs) to confirm the disposal of the 1980's and 1990's WMD. But in order to do that, Bush had to be able to threaten force – the vote made such threats credible. And, as a last resort, if our allies supported us and if it seemed clear Sadaam was empowered with destructive weapons, and if there were no other available options, Kerry agreed war would be necessary. Then, having not wanted the war, once we were in it, he did want to pay for it. He wanted the military to have that $87 billion, and was willing to do the hard work to figure out how to pay for it. It was the administration who wanted to go to war (and did), and the administration who wanted the $87 billion, but did not want to pay for it (which is exactly what happened -- instead of creating a plan to pay for the war sooner rather than later, congress and the administration opted to let future generations pay for our war of choice, figuratively and literally).

Ultimately, the only difference between "a thoughtful, intelligent man" and "a flip-flopper" is perception. If you respect reasoned judgment and intellectual flexibility, you must respect Kerry's thoughtfulness. If you respect stubbornness, sticking to a decision even if it turns out to be wrong, and an insistence on painting every issue in black and white simplicity, despite the complexities of that issue, you'll think him a flip-flopper.

Reason 2:

Kerry can separate personal belief from the greater public good. That is, Kerry respects an individual's right to determine his or her own values and morality. No issue better characterizes this ability than abortion. Kerry is personally, for religious reasons, against abortion – he would not consider abortion as an option for himself or his family, because his Catholic faith does not allow it. That said, he understands that his religious belief is not everyone's and, what's more, that every citizen of this country has the right to determine his or her own religious beliefs. This ability to separate his own faith from the greater good of the self-determination of the American people is an exercise of great personal strength. It is a great human who can hold his or her personal spiritual convictions, which can be stark and zealous, and yet recognize the right of others to do the same, even if their beliefs are in direct opposition to his. Our current president does not have this capacity – his religious convictions, in his mind, should be shared by everyone. Hence, his campaigns against Abortion and gay marriage. These things offend his religious sensibilities, so he wants to make them illegal. Not so with Kerry. Kerry is a religious president we can all live with – one who has deep faith, but does not force his version of good and evil on the rest of us.

Reason 3:

Kerry has plans to try to fix some of what I think is broken in this country, and I think his plans are better than Bush's. His plans for healthcare, the economy, the environment and national security make more sense to me than Bush's plans. His healthcare plan is not perfect: I'm for universal, single-payer healthcare and industry regulation. But it's better than Bush's. His environmental plan is not perfect: his pollution reduction plans are not as aggressive as I'd like, I'd like to see a bigger investment in existing clean energy technologies, and he's still too conciliatory to the fossil fuel industry. But it's a start. And it's better than Bush's. His plan for the economy is not perfect: I'm skeptical he can find a way to pay for all he wants to do. But he's pledged to try a number of new tactics to right our economy, and not to enact a proposal unless he can show how to pay for it. That's a helluva lot better than Bush's plan. And his security plans are not perfect: I think any plan for true national security must include a plan to address worldwide poverty and oppression, which goes far beyond the power of one man, even if that man is the President of the United States. But part of Kerry's plan is a renewed effort to work with other nations toward peace (a real peace, not just Bush's proposed "do what we want and we won't bomb you" shake-down peace), which is certainly better than Bush's.

There it stands. As I see it, this election is not "about the economy, stupid," it's about ideology. If you value stubbornness and feel it is foolish to admit error, if you believe that America should be ruled by a literal biblical Christian morality, if you feel that you want a return to a 1950s social order, and if you think they rest of the world can fuck themselves if they don't like what we do, 'cause we've got the most powerful military in the world, you'll be for George W. Bush. But, if you value careful thought, if you value respect for individual rights, if you value progressive steps in the well-being of American society and, indeed, world society, with some careful research you'll find you want to vote for Kerry.

I know I do.

This Fateful Night

David Nett   November 3, 2004

So, apparently we are a country of "values" and "morals." Time and again I heard that tonight: "in the Midwest, morals are the issue, and the President has the upper hand," and, "in the South, the President's strong values are a key determinant," etc., etc. And, indeed, in those states where "morality" was a top issue, Bush won, and won big. It made me throw up a little in my mouth for, apparently, these are the "morals" and "values" of the United States of America in 2004:

- Homosexuals are second-class (and in Mississippi, where a gay-marriage ban passed 92% to 8%, tenth-class) citizens, worthy of blatant discrimination.

- Putting our soldiers and the entire population of another country at grave risk of death for either gross economic greed, or what amounts to an outright lie (you choose), is a-okay.

- Giving a big "fuck-you" to all the peoples of the world who live outside our border is the way to go.

- Giving a big "fuck-you" to the homeless, the poor, the working-poor and everyone hovering on the brink of poverty within our own country is the way to go.

- Turning our back on the environment is a good idea.

- Ignoring science and human rights in pursuit of a religious ideal and a false hope of security is perfectly reasonable.

Hell, yes, I'm bitter. As I write this, at 12:30AM Pacific Time on November 3, the race is still undecided. CNN has not yet called Ohio, but it looks grim. I don't see us winning this. Even if we manage to squeak an electoral win (and my optimism has melted away), we trail badly in the popular vote, and we end up with an administration without a mandate – 2000 all over again. Yes, it is possible that millions of provisional ballots will turn up, and I will wake up to a pleasant surprise. But I just don't see it. In the end, just by making the thing this close, the conservative right has won this election.

We are a democracy, right or wrong. In this case, I'm afraid, we are badly wrong. Perhaps, though, a loss this year can become a win for the progressive long-term. It will be little consolation to those masses of people, here and abroad, who will be ground under the heel of a second Bush term, but perhaps the wake-up that rural and southern America (for that is who has given Bush victory) needs will be found in the extremely socially and economically damaging policies sure to solidify during a second Bush term. As the next four years grind on, the poor get poorer, the rich get richer, disdain for the United States grows and extends beyond our administration to those who voted to keep it, perhaps those people who continually vote against their own (and society at large's) better interest will be shocked into reality. Perhaps they will realize that wealth and good fortune do not "trickle down," that drilling the entire ANWAR will not make us energy independent, that "preemptive defense" does not make us safer and that state-sanctioned discrimination leads to societal ruin.

Then again, perhaps not. Perhaps we, at large, are like a society of Calvinists, each believing we are predestined to happiness in life and ultimately to heaven, while those who are less fortunate are that through God's design, and they've been predestined for misery, evil and eventually hell since the creation of the world, so why bother trying to make their lives better? Perhaps we believe that we must force our narrow religious morality on a wicked, resistant society because, whatever the short-term cost, we will be rewarded in heaven. I hope, for our sake, there is a heaven ahead for us, for the lives of the average American (who voted in the majority for George Bush), the average Iraqi, the average world citizen are likely to take an unpleasant turn in the short-term, and it will be necessary to have something to look forward to.

Now I'm rambling, and my tiredness betrays my true feelings. I'm sick of this narrow morality which impinges upon the personal and religious freedom of our citizens. I'm sick of a society which turns a blind eye to the ugly and unfortunate. I'm sick of a people who worship the promise of wealth, and ignore every opportunity to help the poor. I'm sick.

And I'm tired. I'm going to bed, to dream of waking to happier news.

In the morning we re-assess our situation, and create our forward-looking plans. Maybe society can't be healed. Maybe we will dissolve in our own selfishness and shortsightedness. But that doesn't mean we can give up. I've got a good job, and I'm likely to keep it (at least in the short term), despite Bush and his policies. I'm one of the lucky ones. It's my other job then, in these next four years, to try to figure out a way to help all those who are less fortunate, and hope, in 2008, they can see clearly enough to help themselves. Being a progressive brings with it an inherent optimism. It's hard to see that tonight, but the daylight will no doubt bring a new perspective, and we will soldier on.

The Day After

David Nett   November 3, 2004

I've been pleased to hear a lot more liberal optimism this morning than I expected. From all corners – my work, my friends, the blogosphere – I hear calls to action, to volunteer, to gear-up and not give up the fight. For that I'm glad. My current misery, my current sense of failure, of "how could we let this happen?" aside, I am in full agreement: we must move forward, redouble our efforts and continue the fight for equality and justice in our society and the world society at large.

One thing I've been hearing that I *don't* like is voice here and there blaming Kerry for this loss. Kerry, while not my first choice, would have been a damn good president. He's a fine man – brave, strong, smart, measured and compassionate. We didn't lose because Kerry wasn't good enough. We lost because, at this point in time, Kerry's (and our) priorities do not match those of 51% of the American people. Kerry, and 48% of us, wanted to make certain everyone got their fair share. Kerry, and 48% of us, wanted to try to close the gap between the rich and the poor, and bring social justice to the downtrodden.

But Bush, and 51% of us, want to make certain fags don't marry, women don't make their own biological decisions, and that brown people in other countries feel the business-end of our military muscle. And that's what it boils down to. Last week I said I think this will come down to ideology, and I was right. In the end, an ideology of fear, hate, and shortsightedness won the day. I don't know how else to put it. Right now, as you can tell, there's a lot of anger oozing around the edges of my vision.

As the days wear on, my bitterness will flake away. Underneath that crusty shell is a renewed desire to make things right in our country, not just for me, but for everyone. I will find a place to volunteer, a place where my skills can be put to good use moving our society forward. I urge you to do the same. I will continue to write and speak my mind, and to do everything I can to protect the idea that we can make this a better place, a more perfect union, by embracing all people, by preserving justice for all, and by holding onto my optimism. I urge you to do the same. That 51% of us – they're scared. They react based upon what they know, and what they know is fear. I'm not a religious person, but I know what, according to Luke and the King James Bible, Jesus said from the cross: "Father, forgive them; for they know not what they do."

That's how I feel about this election. The people have made their decision. The next four years we will have to live with that monumentally flawed decision. But that is no reason to give up on the people. Perhaps, in these next four years, eyes will open, and people will begin to understand why this decision was wrong. And we must be there, to help them understand why justice is important, why equality is a necessity, and how they can help make things right as our country moves forward. Remember, we are not alone. 48% of us agreed yesterday that it is important to try to make things better. Just because election day has passed, those 48% don't go away. We are all still here. And we remain a powerful force for change.

This will be a tough four years. I fear for my gay friends, my female friends, my minority and my friends who live near or below the poverty line. They will bear the brunt of this defeat. And inside I will long feel that I somehow failed them. I'm sure many folks feel the same. But we must take what we have built this past year and move it forward. We must band together, begin fighting and planning now, knowing that while we may not have won today, a new opportunity is just around the corner. We remain Americans, and because our government is based upon democracy, there will always be another chance.

John Kerry just finished his concession speech. He and John Edwards feel the same. Today is hard. It's hard to understand, it's hard to believe, it's hard to accept. But, if we hold on and continue to believe, there is always tomorrow.

How?

Jeanette Scherrer   November 5, 2004

That's the question. How could this happen? How could half of those voters who turned out vote for that lying, smug George Bush? David already covered what we'll get these next four years. I'll tell you how this happened.

I have to accept what this country is, as opposed to what I wish it were. It is a country where most people believe in a god, mostly the Christian god. People like a leader who not only is a vocal Christian, but someone who claims something and makes a decision, even if they disagree with it, as long as that leader stands by their decision and refuses to change his mind no matter what. People like this. How did Bush win? He says things and will not change his mind even if the building is falling down around him. People think this is brave. They don't want Kerry, who studies all sides of a situation and is willing to adjust a plan to new information and situations. No. No change.

What else did Bush do to win? He had people smart enough to know that they had to find what would incite Bush's Christian base to get out and vote. What issues would get them so riled up that they would get off their asses, figure out where their polling places are, grab the keys, get in the car, drive there and vote. Is it Iraq? No. Most people aren't directly effected by it, and they certainly don't give a shit how many innocent Iraqis have and will be killed. Apparently they don't care if they or their children are in danger of a possible draft (oh, and you are by the way, no matter what Bush said). Is it the economy? No. Is it health care? No. What is it?

Moral values. Let me say that again – moral values.

The Republicans not only figured out what the hot issue was, but they knew how to talk about those issues. You have to use fear and speak it like a preacher. Keep it simple and repeat, repeat, repeat. This god-believing country understands the concept of fear, because the bible's overarching teaching is if you don't believe in Jesus you will burn for all eternity. They are comfortable with fear. They understand it. Hmm, now what is a big, passionate hot button of fear for the Christians? Homosexual marriage! The Republican strategists were brilliant to get gay marriage on the ballot in eleven states. That's what got many people out the door. It's clear to me that this is a country that hates homosexuals and would prefer if we were all dead. There are people who, no matter what I did or said, would never change their minds about me. They hate me and don't want to have to accept me as an equal, accept that I was born that way, and especially accept that be being gay is normal. And that's what got them out the door. The opportunity to vote against the fags and dykes marrying brought them out in droves. Did you see all the red in the south? I think it was blood.

OK. I'm not so self absorbed to think that gay marriage was the only hot button. But it's a big one. Abortion. There's another big one. Bush is against abortion and will appoint at least one, if not more, Supreme Court Justice who will want to overturn Roe v. Wade. They know Bush is for abstinence (apparently everyone in the south only has sex after they get married, and then only to procreate). Add to that the intangible fear, thanks to Dick Cheney, that if Kerry wins there will be another terrorist attack. What did someone say? Gays, guns and god. They voted for those moral values before realizing they were unemployed, before realizing they had no health care, before remembering this president has lost more jobs than he's created, before recalling we are involved in war based on lies, before realizing that Bush is a man who has only helped the rich get richer, that his tax cuts won't help them, that they will never, ever be a member of the country club. The point is, people are comfortable with fear. People are not comfortable with change – fear is easier. Fear is known, change is vulnerable.

What can we do? I don't know yet, but I have some ideas for the Democrats. Get some balls. Take homosexual marriage and abortion off the table. Tell people you don't believe in dictating morality. Be direct. Use simple sentences. "Do you want me to tell you how to live your life?" Of course not. "That's right. I trust each individual to do what is right for them while not bringing physical harm to others." About abortion. You say this. "I don't like abortion. Nobody likes abortion. But it should be legal. And you know what? I'm going to focus on girls not getting pregnant in the first place, so I will support comprehensive and frank contraception education in our schools. Would you rather have you girls educated or pregnant?" You just have to say it. You can't and won't get everybody to agree with you. But just say it and stick with it. Say it with some balls. Many will follow and those who don't – fuck 'em.

That's how.

Afterword

On January 20, 2005, George W. Bush will be sworn in for his second term as President of the United States of America.

It's hard not to be deflated by his relatively (compared to 2000) decisive popular victory this second time out. After all the damage he and his have done to our economy, our environment and our position in the world, it's disheartening to know that a majority of Americans want him to try it again.

But it is encouraging to know that after all the writing, all the talking, the convincing, the time spent persuading our friends and family that a second Bush term would be harmful to the United States, that some people *were* swayed. I personally know of three people who, had it not been for some of the hard work we did, would likely have voted for Bush, and instead voted for Kerry. All three were in contested states, which ultimately went for John Kerry. It's possible there were more. My father, for example, despite my devoting an entire eight-part series specifically to changing his mind (and the minds of others like him), will likely never tell me who he voted for – for him, that is private information. My Ma feels the same way. Still, I know for certain we made a small impact.

The world is a scary place right now for Americans and everyone else. President Bush's second term is likley to include an attempt at further erosion of environmental law, a move toward a regressive tax structure, the destruction of Social Security, discrimination against homosexuals, a crusade against reproductive rights, the tacit abolition of the separation of Church and State, and further, possibly long-term, alienation of our friends in the world.

The best thing we can all do in these times is get the word out. The mainstream media are mostly useless in this respect – we cannot expect the evening news or the 24-hour news channels to show the American people the complete picture (we could talk about the degredation of the news media due to corporate greed all day long), nor can we expect the typical American, who is working harder than ever for less and less, to have or take the time to do the research him or herself. Those of us who can parse the information, who have the time, opportunity and desire to sift through piles of opposing opinion and reportage to determine what lies closest to objective reality, need to hold that information up to the light. What I've learned these past four years, and especially this last one, is that it's monumentally difficult to change people's minds. The best thing we can do is make certain, to the best of our ability, that, before people make up their minds, they have as much information as possible, and that the information is as accurate as can be managed. If we all understand the stakes, and the consequences, of our decisions, we're much more likely to do what is best, in the long-term, for ourselves, our country, and our world. We have important federal elections in this country every two years. This means that every two years, and more often on the local level, we can take what we have learned and act to make real, positive democratic change.

You see, in the end I'm still an optimist. I can't promise that I won't spend a lot of time in these next four years cursing the darkness. But you can bet that I will light a candle as well. If enough people do the same, we can bring a lot of light to this world.

David Nett
Editor, Contributor & Webmaster
Clark Schpiell Productions
January 8, 2004

this book would not have been possible
without the following fine folks:

the original CSATFCWB gang
(those whose essays are included in this tome, as well as John
Geiser, Christopher Martinsen, Chris Nett and Eric Schnabel)

Robert Brewer
Steve Files
David Gresham
April Nelson
Craig Nett
Linda Nett
Irena Pereira

and especially
Shannon Nelson

About Us

Clark Schpiell Productions is an online magazine, updated twice weekly, featuring an eclectic blend of essays, humor and art from a dozen or so mildly deranged folks. Check us out at www.clarkschpiell.com.

Craig Bridger is an actor and writer from San Diego, recently transplanted to New York City. While he enjoys the excellent pizza and the great theater, he could do without the ridiculous cold, and the brain-numbing noise.

Joseph G. Carson (aka Jason Groce) is a writer and musician in Seattle, WA. By day he works in a cushy desk job for an unnamed global corporation, but by night he plays in coffee houses throughout the Seattle area under yet another name: Jacob Carver. Find out more about him and his music at www.jacobcarver.com.

Eli Chartkoff is a writer, musician and animator in Los Angeles. Lately, the majority of his time is occupied with raising little Ivan, but you can learn more about his band, the Monolators, at www.themonolators.com, and his animation at www.monsieurgustave.com.

Jeremy Groce went from being a small-town Midwesterner to world traveler (he's lived in seven countries on four continents and speaks a handful of languages), which still surprises him. He runs a shortwave radio station in East Africa, and he and his wife recently welcomed their first child, a beautiful baby girl, into the world.

Nikki Lee is a writer from Toronto, currently residing in Los Angeles, where she slaves away at a dot-com to pay the rent. You can also find her work in *The Shopkeepers*, from Periwinkle Publishers Limited, coming soon to a book store near you.

Michelle Magoffin is a writer in Los Angeles. To pay her crushing mortgage, she works as a producer for a dot-com in Santa Monica. She vents her great angst at botheration.blogspot.com.

David Nett is an actor and a writer in Los Angeles. He's the editor and webmaster of Clark Schpiell Productions, and is on the board (along with his wife, Shannon) of the Lucid by Proxy theater group (www.lucidbyproxy.com). By day, he stares at the walls of a putty-colored cubicle and weeps silently to himself.

Rick Robinson is a writer, actor and director in Los Angeles, and is on the board of Lucid by Proxy as well (along with his wife, Val). To pay his rent, he works as a technical writer for a small software company.

Jeanette Scherrer is a writer, director and actor in Los Angeles, is also on the board of Lucid by Proxy, and makes her ducats as a story editor on various television shows.

Chad Schnaible is an actor and writer in Los Angeles and the winner of the 2002 Dakota Stage Limited Lewis & Clark Playwriting Award. By day, he runs the product placement warehouse for a large P.R. firm, while pining for the life of an international poker superstar.